casenote® Legal Briefs

EVIDENCE

Adaptable to courses utilizing Green and Nesson's casebook on Evidence.

NORMAN S. GOLDENBERG, SENIOR EDITOR
PETER TENEN, MANAGING EDITOR
ROBERT J. SWITZER, ASSOCIATE EDITOR

STAFF WRITERS
Rafael G. Armijo
William Fritz

DISTRIBUTED BY:
LAW DISTRIBUTORS, INC.
14415 S. MAIN STREET
GARDENA, CALIF. 90248

BLISHED BY CASENOTES PUBLISHING CO. INC. P.O. BOX 3946 BEVERLY HILLS, CA 90212
84S

FORMAT
FOR
THE CASENOTE LEGAL BRIEF

The following outline indicates the organization of a Casenote Legal Brief:

NATURE OF CASE: **This section indicates the** *form of action* **(i.e., breach of contract, negligence, battery, etc.), the** *type of proceeding* **(i.e., demurrer, appeal from trial court's jury instructions, etc.) and the** *relief sought* **(i.e., damages, injunction, criminal sanctions, etc.).**

FACT SUMMARY: **The fact summary is included merely to** *refresh the student's memory.* **It is assumed that the student has already read the complete discussion of the facts and is familiar with them. This section is therefore not a complete and thorough presentation of the facts. It can be used to quickly recall the facts of the opinion when the student is chosen by an instructor to brief a case.**

CONCISE RULE OF LAW: **This portion of the brief, like the fact summary, is included to** *refresh the student's memory.* **This section is not intended to provide a full presentation of the rule and rationale in the case. Rather it should be used for instant recall of the court's holding and for classroom discussion or home review.**

FACTS: Here the editors present a precise expression of all *relevant facts* of the case including the contentions of the parties and lower court holdings. It is written in a logical order to enable the student to have a clear understanding of the case. The plaintiff and defendant are indicated by their proper names throughout and are always labeled with a (P) or (D).

ISSUE: The issue is a *concise question which brings out the essence of the opinion* as it relates to the section of the book in which it appears. Both substantive and procedural issues are included if relevant to the decision.

HOLDING AND DECISION: This section offers a clear and in-depth discussion of the *rule of the case and the court's rationale.* It is written in easy-to-understand language. When relevant, the student is provided with a thorough discussion of the exceptions listed by the court, the concurring and dissenting opinions, and the names of the judges.

EDITOR'S ANALYSIS: This addition to the brief is a new innovation. It is a Horn-book style discussion of how the case is relevant to the section of the book and to the entire course. It indicates whether the case is a majority or minority opinion. It compares the principle case with other cases in the casebook. It also provides analysis from restatements, uniform codes, legal encyclopedias and treatises. This section points out the history of the case, the type of transaction involved and ways to avoid problems the case presents for the lawyer. In other words, it gives the student a broad understanding of *where the case "fits in" with other cases in the section of the book and with the entire course.* The editor's analysis will prove to be invaluable to classroom discussion.

EDITOR'S NOTE: **Casenote Legal Briefs** ***are intended to supplement the student's casebook, not replace it. The student must master the skill of briefing if he/she expects to succeed in the study of law. There is no substitute for the student's own mastery of this important learning and study technique. If used properly,*** **Casenote Legal Briefs** ***are an effective law study aid which serve to reinforce the student's understanding of the cases.***

NOTE TO THE STUDENT

It is the goal of Casenotes Publishing Company, Inc. to create and distribute the finest, clearest and most accurate legal briefs available. To this end, we are constantly seeking new ideas, comments and constructive criticism. As a user of Casenote Legal Briefs, your suggestions will be highly valued. With all correspondence, please include your complete name, address, and telephone number, including area code and zip code.

Casenote Legal Briefs are printed on perforated, three-hole punched sheets for easy inclusion in ringed binders. To remove a page, first fold the page at the perforations and then tear the sheet using care not to rip the punched holes.

It's also easy to save the valuable reference glossary of common Latin words and phrases and French derivatives, which appears on the inside front and rear covers of your *Casenote Legal Briefs*. Simply remove the covers by cutting along the line printed near the spine of the book and place them in your three-ring binder.

REF. # 1065-83-84-685

SUPPLEMENT REQUEST FORM

At the time this book was printed, a brief was included for every major case in the casebook and for every existing supplement to the casebook. However, if a new supplement to the casebook (or a new edition of the casebook) has been published since this publication was printed and if that casebook supplement (or new edition of the casebook) was available for sale at the time you purchased this Casenote Legal Briefs book, we will be pleased to provide you the new cases contained therein AT NO CHARGE when you send us a stamped, self-addressed envelope.

TO OBTAIN YOUR FREE SUPPLEMENT MATERIAL, **YOU MUST FOLLOW THE INSTRUCTIONS BELOW PRECISELY** OR REQUEST WILL NOT BE ACKNOWLEDGED!

1. Please check if there is in fact an existing supplement and, if so, that the cases are not already included in your Casenote Legal Briefs. Check the main table of cases as well as the supplement table of cases, if any.

2. *REMOVE THIS ENTIRE PAGE FROM THE BOOK.* You MUST send this ORIGINAL page to receive your supplement. This page acts as your proof of purchase and contains the reference number necessary to fill your supplement request properly. No photocopy of this page or written request will be honored or answered. Any request from which the reference number has been removed, altered or obliterated will not be honored.

3. Prepare a STAMPED self-addressed envelope for return mailing. Be sure to use a FULL SIZE (9 × 12) ENVELOPE (MANILA TYPE) so that the supplement will fit, and AFFIX ENOUGH POSTAGE TO COVER 3 OZ. **ANY SUPPLEMENT REQUEST NOT ACCOMPANIED BY A STAMPED SELF-ADDRESSED ENVELOPE WILL ABSOLUTELY NOT BE FILLED OR ACKNOWLEDGED.**

4. MULTIPLE SUPPLEMENT REQUESTS: If you are ordering more than one supplement, we suggest that you enclose a stamped, self-addressed envelope for each supplement requested. If you enclose only one envelope for a multiple request, your order may not be filled immediately should any supplement which you requested still be in production. In other words, your order will be held by us until it can be filled completely.

5. CASENOTES prints two kinds of supplements. A "*New Edition*" supplement is issued when a new edition of your casebook is published. A "*New Edition*" supplement gives you all major cases found in the new edition of the casebook which did not appear in the previous edition. A regular "*supplement*" is issued when a paperback supplement to your casebook is published. If the box at the lower right is stamped, then the "*New Edition*" supplement was provided to your bookstore and is *not* available from CASENOTES, however CASENOTES will still send you any regular "*supplements*" which have been printed either before or after the new edition of your casebook appeared and which, according to the reference number at the top of this page, have not been included in this book. If the box is not stamped, CASENOTES will send you any supplements, "*New Edition*" and/or regular, needed to completely update your Casenote Legal Briefs.

6. Fill in the following information:

   A. Full title of CASEBOOK ______________________

   ____

   B. CASEBOOK author's name ______________________

   ____

   C. Date of new supplement which you are requesting ______

   D. Name and location of bookstore where this *Casenote Legal Briefs* was purchased

   ____

   ____

   E. Name and location of law school you attend ______

   ____

   F. Any comments regarding *Casenote Legal Briefs* ______

   ____

   ____

NOTE: IF THIS BOX IS STAMPED, NO *NEW EDITION* SUPPLEMENT CAN BE OBTAINED BY MAIL.

CASENOTES PUBLISHING, CO., INC.   P.O. Box 3946   Beverly Hills, CA 90212-0946

PLEASE PRINT

NAME ______________________ **PHONE( )** ______________________

ADDRESS/CITY/STATE/ZIP ______________________

TABLE OF CASES

TABLE OF CASES — 1984 SUPPLEMENT

ROMANO v. ANN & HOPE FACTORY OUTLET, INC.

417 A.2d 1375 (R.I. 1980)

NATURE OF CASE: Appeal from directed verdict denying damages for personal injuries.

FACT SUMMARY: Romano (P), who brought suit for personal injuries received in a bicycle accident allegedly caused by a defective brake mechanism, appealed from a directed verdict against her.

CONCISE RULE OF LAW: When the relevancy of proffered evidence is dependent upon a preliminary fact, it is the responsibility of the trial judge to make determinations as to the existence or non-existence of the underlying preliminary fact.

FACTS: Romano (P) was injured in a bicycle accident when the brakes on her bicycle failed as she was coasting down a hill. The bike was purchased from Ann & Hope (D). Romano (P) claimed the brake failure resulted from its defective design, which allowed a loss of oil and the presence of dust in the brake chamber. Mandell, a consulting engineer, examined the bike approximately two years after the accident and made findings as to the cause of the brake failure which supported Romano's (P) claims. Romano (P) brought suit and offered Mandell's expert testimony as to the condition of the brake mechanism. In response to objections from counsel for Ann & Hope (D), Romano (P) sought to show that there had been no substantial change in the condition of the bicycle from the time of the accident to the time of Mandell's examination. Testimony revealed that after the accident, the bicycle was stored in the workroom of Romano's (P) home for a short time until delivered to Costerus, a mechanical engineer, who then tested the brake mechanism. He never found a total loss of braking power,nor did he disassemble or lubricate the braking mechanism. A few weeks later, the bicycle was returned to Romano's (P) storeroom, where it remained until Mandell's examination. No testimony was received as to the conditions present in the storeroom. Counsel for Ann & Hope (D) continued to object, and the trial judge, unconvinced that Romano (P) had sufficiently established that there had been no substantial change in the condition of the bicycle, refused to admit the testimony of Mandell, and directed a verdict in favor of Ann & Hope (D), from which Romano (P) appealed.

ISSUE: When the relevancy of proffered evidence is dependent upon a preliminary fact, is it the responsibility of the trial judge to make determinations as to the existence or non-existence of the underlying preliminary fact?

HOLDING AND DECISION: (Kelleher, J.) Yes. The doctrine of conditional relevancy, which would submit preliminary fact questions to the jury on a prima facie showing of the existence of the preliminary fact, is not embraced here. The trial judge must exercise discretion regarding the admissibility of evidence when there has been an objection of relevancy. When the relevancy of the proffered evidence is dependent upon a preliminary fact, it is the responsibility of the trial judge to make determinations as to the existence or non-existence of the preliminary fact. Here, evidentiary rulings as to the similarity of conditions proved and at issue are within the scope of the trial judge's discretion. Given that no testimony was received as to the conditions of storage, and the effect of the tests performed by Costerus on the condition of the bicycle cannot be determined, it cannot be concluded that the trial judge committed reversible error in refusing to admit Mandell's testimony. As a matter of discretion, he could have concluded that the condition of the brake when examined by Mandell was not substantially the same as it was at the time of the accident. Affirmed and remanded.

EDITOR'S ANALYSIS: Under the doctrine of conditional relevance, where the court makes a determination of the prima facie showing of the existence of a preliminary fact, the court is restricted to using that evidence that the jury has before it in making the determination, that is on evidence that has been properly admitted under the rules of error in force. If the judge finds that the prima facie showing of the preliminary fact has not been made, he must then instruct the jury to disregard the testimony and evidence used in the attempt to make the showing.

NOTES:

UNITED STATES v. GRASSI

602 F.2d 1192 (5th Cir. 1979), vacated and remanded on other grounds, 448 U.S. 902 (1980)

NATURE OF CASE: Appeal from conviction for interstate transportation of obscene materials.

FACT SUMMARY: Grassi (D) appealed his conviction for interstate transportation of obscene materials, claiming prejudicial error in the trial court's allowing the prosecution to show films to the jury to prove obscenity, even after defense counsel had offered to stipulate to the obscenity of the films in question.

CONCISE RULE OF LAW: Determining the weight to be given an offer to stipulate in the balancing of the probative value of a particular piece of evidence against its prejudicial effect lies within the sound discretion of the trial court.

FACTS: Grassi (D) was indicted for interstate transportation of obscene materials for his part in the distribution of five films. The prosecution asked permission to show the films to the jury to prove the obscenity element of the crime charged. Objecting to the prejudicial effect showing the films would have on his client, counsel for Grassi (D) offered to stipulate to the films' obscenity. The prosecution refused to accept the stipulation, and the trial court partially overruled Grassi's (D) objection, allowing the jury to see three of the films. The films portrayed bizarre and repulsive sex acts, but the films were also largely repititious in nature. Grassi (D) was convicted, and appealed on the grounds that given the offer to stipulate, the films should have been excluded since their probative value was substantially outweighed by their prejudicial effect.

ISSUE: Does the weight to be given to an offer to stipulate in the balancing of the probative value of a particular piece of evidence against its prejudicial effect lie within the sound discretion of the trial court?

HOLDING AND DECISION: (Clark, J.) Yes. Determining the weight to be given an offer to stipulate in the balancing of the probative value of a particular piece of evidence against its prejudicial effect lies within the sound discretion of the trial court. In this balancing process, the court has to weigh the probative value of the evidence and the proponent's need for the evidence against the unfair prejudice (the undue tendency to suggest a decision on an improper basis) that will result from its admission. To argue that an offer to stipulate requires exclusion of the evidence allows the party offering to stipulate to control the proof presented at trial and robs the evidence of its moral force. To say that the probative value of a piece of evidence necessary to prove an element of a crime can never be substantially outweighed by its prejudicial effect even if there has been an offer to stipulate means that the prosecution could never be required to accept a defendent's stipulations. Both approaches ignore precedent and achieve undesired results. The trial court, in exercising its discretion on a case-by-case basis, should attempt to achieve fundamental fairness in the trial, and can thus accept or reject the tendered stipulation, in whole or in part. In the contest of this case, the trial court did not abuse its discretion in allowing the jury to see three of the films. The probative value of the films was substantial, even in light of the offered stipulation, and there was no cumulative prejudicial effect since the films, after their initial shock value, were repetitive to the point of boredom. Affirmed.

EDITOR'S ANALYSIS: The offer to stipulate should be given considerable weight in the balancing process. Acceptance of an offer to stipulate can significantly reduce the time required to establish elements in a case that are not really at issue, and diminishes the potential for undue prejudice. Where the probative value or moral force of the evidence is not great, a party should be required to accept the stipulation.

NOTES:

STATE v. POE

SUPREME CT. OF UTAH, 1968. 21 Utah 2d 113, 441 P.2d 512 Appl. after remand. 24 Utah 2d 355, 471 P.2d 870

NATURE OF CASE: Appeal from conviction of first degree murder.

FACTUAL SUMMARY: At his trial, where he was charged with murdering a lifelong resident of a small community, Poe (D) objected to the composition of the jury and the showing of gruesome, colored slides of the victim's autopsy to the jury.

CONCISE RULE OF LAW: Although it is within the sound discretion of the trial court to determine whether the inflammatory nature of offered visual evidence is outweighed by its probative value with respect to a fact in issue, it may not be admitted if all the material facts which could conceivably have been adduced had been established by other uncontradicted evidence or testimony.

FACTS: Poe (D) was charged with murdering a lifelong resident of a small community of some 10,000 residents. Members of the jury were acquainted with the sheriff, some of the witnesses for the prosecution, the victim, the defendant, and the prosecutors. The trial court admitted into evidence black and white photographs showing the victim lying in his bed in a sleeping position, with two bullet holes in his head. It also admitted colored slides taken during the course of the autopsy. Poe's (D) counsel failed to make the proper objection at this point to the admission of the slides. The colored slides accentuated the gruesomeness of the autopsy. Poe (D) was convicted, the jury not recommending life imprisonment. On appeal, Poe (D) challenged the "community pattern of thought as expressed by potential jurors," and the introduction of the slides as being needlessly inflammatory with little probative value.

ISSUE: (1) Is the fact that potential jurors are well-acquainted with the victim and various witnesses for the prosecution sufficient to establish a denial of a fair trial?

(2) Should inflammatory evidence be excluded if all of the conclusions which could have been made from the inflammatory evidence were established by other evidence?

HOLDING AND DECISION: (1) No. The trial judge had carefully and exhaustively examined the jury panel. Furthermore, the panel had been passed for cause by the defendant. There is no direct evidence that the acquaintanceships of the prospective jurors to the victim and the witnesses were prejudicial to Poe (D). (2) Yes. The colored slides had no probative value since independent testimony had established all the facts which could have been adduced from viewing them. Their only purpose was to inflame and arouse the jury. The slides could very well have tipped the scales in favor of the death penalty. Even though Poe's (D) counsel did not raise the proper objection, the court will overlook the technicality. The case is reversed and remanded for a new trial.

DISSENT: All evidence given tends to prejudice the jury, but otherwise competent evidence which a witness could testify to should be admissible. If the defendant wished to avoid having the jury see the pictures, he could have stipulated to the cause of death. These pictures were no more gruesome than was the openheart surgery portrayed on television.

EDITOR'S ANALYSIS: A photograph is admitted usually under the theory that it is only a graphic portrayal of oral testimony to which a witness must lay the appropriate foundation. However, the vividness of colored photographs and motion pictures often leaves too strong an impression on the jury. Preliminary viewing of the film or a photograph may be done by the trial court. McCormick suggests that the difficulty posed in this regard may be diminished today by more sophisticated moviegoing jurors.

NOTES:

PEOPLE v. COLLINS

Sup. Ct. of Ca., 1968. 68 Cal. 2d 319, 66 Cal. Rptr. 497, 438 P.2d 33, noted 48 Ore. L.Rev. 281 (1969)

NATURE OF CASE: Appeal from conviction of second degree robbery.

FACT SUMMARY: Prosecutor presented probability statistics at trial suggesting that there was but one chance in 12 million that any couple possessing the characteristics of the Collins' (D) had committed the robbery in question.

CONCISE RULE OF LAW: The use of mathematical techniques in the proof of facts, particularly in a criminal case, must be critically examined in view of the substantial unfairness to a defendant which may result from ill conceived techniques with which the trier of fact is not technically equipped to cope.

FACTS: An eyewitness to a purse-snatching informed police that a caucasion girl with blond hair and a ponytail had committed the robbery and had then driven off in a yellow car driven by a male, bearded negro. Mr. and Mrs. Collins (D) fit this general description except that at the time of their arrest Mr. Collins (D) did not have a beard, claiming to have shaved it off earlier, and Mrs. Collins (D) had somewhat darker hair. At trial, the prosecutor had difficulty in establishing positive eyewitness identification. He thereupon called a professor of mathematics. The prosecutor asked this witness to assume probability factors for the various characteristics which he, the prosecutor, deemed to be shared by the guilty couple. The professor then stated that, from his calculations, there was but one chance in 12 million that any couple possessed the distinctive characteristics of the Collins' (D). The prosecutor then urged the jury to infer that there could be but one chance in 12 million that the Collins (D) were innocent. The Collins (D) were convicted of second degree robbery.

ISSUE: Is the use of mathematical techniques by a prosecutor in a criminal case grounds for error if it is distracting, or confusing to the jury?

HOLDING AND DECISION: Yes. Because jurors who may be unduly impressed by the mystique of a mathematical demonstration may also be unable to assess its relevance or value, a court must closely scrutinize the offered evidence in terms of unfairness to the defendant in a criminal case. In the present case, the record is completely devoid of any evidence relating to any of the probability factors used by the prosecutor and ascribed by him to the six characteristics (i.e. that only one out of every 10 girls who might have been at the scene of the robbery wore a pigtail). Nor was any proof presented that the characteristics selected were mutually independent (i.e. Negroes with beards and men with mustaches represent overlapping categories). More crucially, the approach could furnish the jury with absolutely no guidance on the critical issue: of the admittedly few such couples, which one, if any, was guilty of committing this robbery? The prosecution's eyewitness could have confused a light skinned Negress with bleached hair for a Caucasion blonde, or a bearded driver for one wearing a false beard as a disguise. Finally, statistical analysis simply does not lead to the conclusion that the Collins were probably the guilty couple; the analysis does not prove that no other bearded Negro in the area drove a yellow car accompanied by a ponytailed blonde. A jury could not have remotely begun to comprehend the myriad subtleties of this sophisticated, and confusing, analysis. The conviction is reversed.

EDITOR'S ANALYSIS: McCormick cautions against reading the Collins decision as an end to all further attempts to utilize statistical, or probability analysis during a trial: "Although the court treated the task of combining numerical or non-numerical probabilities as extremely difficult for the average juror (and defense counsel), it can hardly have meant it was impossible in every case. The facts which experts are asked to treat as true in a hypothetical question are frequently themselves in great doubt; and to hold that they must be conclusively established before the expert can quote any number himself would be to upset many decided cases." McCormack on Evidence (2d Ed. 1972) §204, b. 494-495.

NOTES:

ROBBINS v. FARMERS UNION GRAIN TERMINAL ASSN.

522 F.2d 788 (8th Cir. 1977)

NATURE OF CASE: Appeal from award of damages in products liability case.

FACT SUMMARY: Farmers Union (D) appealed from an award of damages in a products liability case on the grounds that a letter representing a subsequent remedial warning was improperly admitted by the trial court.

CONCISE RULE OF LAW: Evidence of subsequent remedial warnings is admissible as substantive evidence in a strict liability action.

FACTS: Robbins (P) was a partner in a cattle feeding operation. In the fall of 1971, they purchased a number of calves and started them on a feeding program which included Rum-Liq, a feed supplement manufactured by Farmers Union (D). The Rum-Liq was a feed supplement containing a high level of urea. The Rum-Liq purchased by Robbins (P) bore a warning that cattle coming into a feed lot should be given 10 days to adjust to the stress before starting them on a full feeding program. Robbins (P) started the cattle on 1/4 pound of Rum-Liq daily, gradually increasing the dosage so that after 14 days of conditioning, the cattle were receiving one pound of Rum-Liq daily. In December 1971, after a number of cattle had become sick and had died, two calves were examined. A high level of ammonia was found in their blood, and Robbins (P) was advised that this could be a result of urea feeding. Robbins (P) stopped Rum-Liq feeding immediately, and the death and sickness among his cattle decreased rapidly. Robbins (P) sued Farmers Union (D), alleging that Farmers Union (D) failed to give adequate warnings for the safe use of Rum-Liq, in that they should have known that experts recommended a longer delay than 10 days before starting calves on a full feeding program. Robbins (P) sought to introduce a letter of subsequent remedial warning by Farmers Union (D) to its sales personnel under strict liability to show an unreasonably dangerous product, and under a negligence theory to show the feasibility of issuing the subsequent warning earlier. Farmers Union (D) was found liable and appealed on the grounds that the letter of subsequent remedial warning was improperly admitted by the trial court.

ISSUE: Is evidence of subsequent remedial warnings admissible as substantive evidence in a strict liability action?

HOLDING AND DECISION: (Lay, J.) Yes. Evidence of subsequent remedial warnings is admissible as substantive evidence in a strict liability action. The exclusionary rule governing subsequent remedial measures is applicable by its terms only to negligence or culpable conduct, and serves no anti-deterent purpose in a strict liability action, since the defendent's culpability is not in question. This rationale has been extended to apply to proof of post-occurence design modification and subsequent remedial instructions. Therefore, if the evidence can be shown to be relevant, it should be admissible. Here, the subsequent remedial warning could be used as substantive evidence on the causation and unreasonably dangerous product elements of a strict liability cause of action, and was therefore properly admitted. Since Farmers Union (D) did not specifically object to the failure of the trial court to give a limiting instruction, the fact that the evidence was inadvertently admitted generally does not require reversal. Affirmed.

EDITOR'S ANALYSIS: The view in this case is representative of the trend in products liability cases away from the general rule of exclusion of evidence of subsequent remedial measures. While commentators have attempted to distinguish products liability cases from negligence cases, the likely reasons for the departure from th rule seem to be the desire to spread losses, and the notion that the policy behind the rule, that exclusion will encourage people to take remedial steps, is simply not applicable to large corporate manufacturers.

NOTES:

WERNER v. UPJOHN CO.

628 F.2d 848 (4th Cir. 1980)

NATURE OF CASE: Appeal from award of damages for negligence.

FACT SUMMARY: Upjohn (D) appealed an award of damages in a negligence action for injuries Werner (P) received as a result of taking a prescription drug manufactured by Upjohn (D).

CONCISE RULE OF LAW: Even if a suit contains a strict liability claim, evidence of a subsequent remedial warning cannot be used to prove antecedent negligence or culpable conduct.

FACTS: Upjohn (D) was the manufacturer of the drug Cleocin. The use of Cleocin was found to have a number of serious side effects, most notably severe diarrhea and colitus. Warning information as to these side effects accompanied shipments of Cleocin. Werner (P) went to a doctor in 1974 for the treatment of an eye condition and prescribed Cleocin. Werner (P) received injuries as a result of taking the drug, and brought suit against Upjohn (D) under theories of negligence and stict liability. A central issue was the adequacy of the warning that accompanied Cleocin in 1975. Upjohn (D) sought to exclude all reference to the subsequent warning, but it was admitted to the jury on the issue of feasibility, even though it was used in witness examination and closing arguement to show what Upjohn (D) should have done. Werner (P) prevailed and was awarded damages, and Upjohn (D) appealed.

ISSUE: Can evidence of a subsequent remedial warning be used to prove antecedent negligence or culpable conduct where the suit contains a strict liability claim?

HOLDING AND DECISION: (Widener, J.) No. Even if a suit contains a strict liability claim, evidence of a subsequent remedial warning cannot be used to prove antecedent negligence or culpable conduct. Courts have split on this issue, and a majority of courts would admit this type of evidence. The rules which bar evidence of subsequent remedial measures to prove negligence or culpable conduct simply do not speak to the issue of whether such evidence should be admitted in a strict liability action. The distinction between negligence actions, which focus on the defendant, and strict liability, which focuses on the product, is of little significance in failure to warn cases, since the issue in both types of cases is essentially the same: was the warning adequate? The policy behind the exclusionary rule, that by excluding this evidence defendants will be encouraged to make improvements, would seem applicable in both negligence and strict liability actions. In this case, while the evidence was admitted solely for the jury's consideration of the issue of feasibility, Werner's (P) use of the warning to show what Upjohn (D) should have done can only be characterized as a use to show negligence, and should have therefore been excluded, even though a strict liability claim was also involved. Judgment vacated; case remanded for a new trial.

EDITOR'S ANALYSIS: Some of the ways in which subsequent remedial measures may be used in a negligence action are to show ownership, control, or as in the present case, the feasibility of a precautionary measure. The purpose for which the subsequent remedial measure is brought in must be controverted, and if the party against whom the evidence is offered chooses to concede the issue, the evidence is inadmissible.

NOTES:

PEOPLE v. ZACKOWITZ

CT. OF APPLS., N.Y.1939. 172 N.E.466, 254 N.Y. 192

NATURE OF CASE: Prosecution for first degree murder.

FACT SUMMARY: The decedent insulted Zackowitz's (D) wife and Zackowitz (D) later, while in a rage and under the influence of alcohol, shot and killed him.

CONCISE RULE OF LAW: Character is never an issue in a criminal prosecution unless the defendant chooses to make it one.

FACTS: Coppola, the decedent, was one of four men who insulted Zackowitz's (D) wife. Zackowitz (D) threatened to kill them if they did not leave within five minutes. Zackowitz (D) walked his wife home where she told him that the men had propositioned her. Zackowitz (D) had been drinking and went into a rage. He either armed himself with a pistol or had previously been carrying one (he offered two different stories, the latter one at trial) and went back to see if the men were still there. There were words and a fight during which Zackowitz (D) shot Coppola. Zackowitz (D) left the scene and was subsequently arrested about two months later. The question at trial was Zackowitz's (D) state of mind. Was the murder premeditated or was it done in the heat of a liquor induced rage (second degree murder)? The prosecution was allowed to introduce, over Zackowitz's (D) objection, testimony showing that Zackowitz (D) owned three other pistols and a tear gas gun. These weapons had been obtained prior to the shooting and there was no claim made that they were carried by Zackowitz (D) when he shot Coppola. The evidence was introduced to show that Zackowitz (D) was "a desperate type of criminal," a "person criminally inclined." Zackowitz (D) was convicted of first degree murder.

ISSUE: Should a defendant's guilt of a specific crime be inferrable from his general character?

HOLDING AND DECISION: No. It is a fundamental rule that character is never an issue in a criminal prosecution unless the defendant chooses to make it one. In a very real sense, a defendant starts his life anew. His guilt must be established with regard to the particular crime with which he is charged. The law has made a policy decision to exclude evidence of this nature in order to protect the innocent. "The natural and inevitable tendency of the tribunal – whether judge or jury – is to give excessive weight to the vicious record of crime thus exhibited, and either to allow it to bear too strongly on the present charge, or to take the proof of it as justifying a condemnation irrespective of guilt of the present charge." The evidence of the hidden guns would be admissible if they had been purchased subsequent to Zackowitz's (D) wife being insulted in order to show motive or design, or if Zackowitz (D) had been carrying all of them (act of preparation). However, the fact that Zackowitz (D) had the guns at home does not tend to prove, even inferentially, his murder of Coppola was premeditated. Ownership of weapons was not relevant to the charge.

DISSENT: The possession of these weapons was a separate crime. The people may prove other crimes against the defendant in a criminal prosecution if such proof tends to establish (1) motive; (2) intent; (3) absence of mistake or accident; (4) common scheme or plan embracing two or more crimes so related to one another that proof of one tends to establish the other; (5) the identity of the person charged with the crime. The weapons have a bearing on the crime in general. If Zackowitz (D) had been carrying them at the time of the murder such evidence would have been admissible. The fact that they were a short distance away in his apartment should not make a difference. Zackowitz (D) was presented to the jury as a man having dangerous weapons in his possession, making a selection from them and then going out to kill those whom he previously had threatened. The prosecution did not seek to introduce the evidence as to general character, but to show that Zackowitz (D), having the means and opportunity to carry out his threat, proceeded to do so.

EDITOR'S ANALYSIS: Aside from the prejudicial nature of character evidence in criminal prosecutions is the question of its probative value. If its introduction will not prove one of the elements of the crime charged, is it really relevant? Does the fact that Zackowitz (D) had weapons available prove, either directly or inferentially, that the killing was premeditated? If it does, why can't the same reasoning apply to anyone owning a single handgun, switchblade, etc.? The question here is whether Zackowitz (D) had a rational intent to murder Coppola prior to the commission of the killing. Does the fact that he had a weapon or weapons at home bear any relevance to intent? The law has made it a general policy that what a party was or had previously done (with the exception of the five points listed by the Dissent) is not relevant to the current charges against him. If the defendant introduces testimony as to his good character, the prosecution may rebut by introducing evidence as to his past crimes, misconduct, or reputation. So, while a defendant in a criminal prosecution may always introduce testimony as to his good character, he does so at the risk of allowing the prosecution to introduce contrary evidence of a like nature. The rationale is that the prosecution always has the right to rebut direct testimony and the fact that this would prejudice defendant is irrelevant.

NOTES:

UNITED STATES v. DANZEY

594 F.2d 905 (2d.Cir. 1979)

NATURE OF CASE: Appeal from robbery conviction.

FACT SUMMARY: Evidence of trademark methods (modus operandi) used in a series of robberies was presented by the government (P) at the beginning of the trial over Gore's (D) objection that its presentation at that stage of the trial was unfairly prejudicial.

CONCISE RULE OF LAW: Ordinarily, modus operandi evidence can be introduced in the government's case-in-chief if the evidence is relevant to identity, but not if the evidence is relevant to intent.

FACTS: Gore (D) admitted that he had used trademark methods in robberies that he had committed four months before and after the robbery in question which included working with two or three accomplices, walking with an ape-like gait while robbing a bank, using a get-away car stolen the night before which was opposite in color to a switching car, and always committing his robberies between 9:00 and 11:00 a.m. The only evidence showing that Gore (D) was the one committing the robbery in question was a witness observing his methods while inside the bank, another witness parked outside of the bank observing his mannerisms when he fled the bank after the robbery in a white car, and a third witness observing him switch from a white to a gold car several blocks from the robbery near the approximate time of the robbery. Gore (D) objected to the admission of his statements describing his methods used in other robberies as being more prejudicial than probative, and to the use of his statements in the government's (P) case-in-chief rather than after he had presented his defense.

ISSUE: When the only major issue is the identity of the criminal, and the government has only modus operandi evidence to prove identity in its case-in-chief, may relevant modus operandi evidence be presented to prove identity in the government's case-in-chief?

HOLDING AND DECISION: (J. Oakes) Yes. As long as the modus operandi evidence is relevant to the crime charged and is used to prove that the defendant is the person observed committing the crime, the modus operandi evidence may be introduced at the beginning of the trial in the government's case-in-chief. Modus operandi evidence presented here of other similar acts closely parallelled the acts witnessed in the crime at issue and occurred in times proximate to the time at which the crime at issue occurred. It is thus clearly relevant. Past similar acts described in Gore's (D) statements were admitted to prove that Gore (D) intentionally, rather than accidentally, robbed the bank. Because of the highly prejudicial nature of modus operandi evidence, such evidence used to prove intent is admissible only to rebut a defendant's claim that criminal intent was lacking because the acts were accidental. When modus operandi evidence is used to prove identity, however, it can be introduced at any time after its relevance is established whether or not the defendant denies allegations of identity.

EDITOR'S ANALYSIS: In light of the highly prejudicial nature of modus operandi evidence, the court's allowance of it at the beginning of the trial seems harsh. It is probably ineffective to instruct the jury that the evidence is meant to show only the identity of the criminal and not to be considered when forming opinions about the defendant's character. However, the requirement of showing that modus operandi evidence is closely relevant to the criminal acts at issue serves as a substantial safeguard protecting the defendant from unfair prejudice against the defendant's character and propensity to act in certain ways.

NOTES:

TUCKER v. STATE

SUPREME CT. OF NEVADA, 1966. 82 NEV. 127, 412 P.2d 970

NATURE OF CASE: Prosecution for second degree murder.

FACT SUMMARY: Tucker (D) woke up to find that Evans was dead on Tucker's (D) sofa, a situation which was quite similar to an event which had happened to Tucker (D) six years earlier.

CONCISE RULE OF LAW: A criminal defendant must have committed the independent offense which is sought to be introduced by the prosecution.

FACTS: In 1957, Tucker (D) awoke to find the body of Kaylor in Tucker's (D) dining room. The case was investigated by the police and a grand jury was convened, but no indictment was returned. In 1963, Tucker (D) awoke to find Evans dead on his sofa (shot to death). This time he was indicted. At the trial, evidence was admitted concerning the earlier death of Kaylor because of the striking similarity between the two deaths. Tucker (D) was convicted of second degree murder.

ISSUE: Can evidence be introduced of a prior crime although the defendant was never convicted of it?

HOLDING AND DECISION: No. There is nothing in the record to establish that Tucker (D) killed Kaylor. Anonymous crimes have no relevance in deciding whether the defendant committed the crime for which he was charged. The court adopted the rule that, "before evidence of a collateral offense is admissible for any purpose, the prosecution must first establish by plain, clear and convincing evidence, that the defendant committed that offense. Fundamental fairness demands this standard in order to preclude verdicts which might otherwise rest on false assumptions." The prosecution had introduced the evidence because of the parallel circumstances between the deaths of Kaylor and Evans on the assumption that these showed a common scheme or purpose. However, without a showing that Tucker (D) was guilty of the first killing, there is no way in which a jury could draw the common scheme inference. Because of its prejudicial nature, its introduction was reversible error.

EDITOR'S ANALYSIS: Usually evidence which shows a common plan, design or system is admissible to show one link in a chain of events which constitutes or at least indicates the commission of the crime charged. There must be a reasonable similarity showing a modus operandi from which the jury could logically infer that the commission of the earlier crime tends to show that the defendant was likely to have committed the crime charged. Therefore, in a case such as Lyles v. State, 215 Ga. 229, 109 S.E. 2d 785 (1959), the court allowed evidence to be introduced that the defendant had previously murdered two husbands and a mother-in-law. These three plus Lyles' daughter (the crime she was being charged with) were all killed by arsenic poisoning; were close family members leaving insurance naming Lyles as a beneficiary; Lyles predicted all of their deaths and expressed a dislike of all of them, etc. While nearly a perfect example of prior similar crimes, Lyles does point out the type of parallel circumstances the court is looking for. Without them, a jury cannot logically bridge the inferential gap between the proved commission of past misdeeds and current misconduct. And, where the past misconduct has not been proved, any inferences drawn must be based on suspicion and innuendo. These types of inferences will not be allowed because the jury would have to infer the commission of the previous misdeed, a collateral issue not before the court.

NOTES:

PEOPLE v. MASSEY

DIST.CT.OF APP.OF CAL., 1961. 196 Cal.App.2d 230, 16 Cal.Rptr.402

NATURE OF CASE: Appeal from conviction for burglary.

NOTES:

FACT SUMMARY: At the trial evidence was introduced of a second burglary which occurred in the same neighborhood as the burglary on trial. Massey (D) had been charged with and acquitted of the second burglary.

CONCISE RULE OF LAW: An acquittal does not prevent the admissibility of evidence concerning another wrongful act, since conviction of the offense is not a prerequisite to the introduction of such evidence.

FACTS: At Massey's (D) trial for burglary, evidence of another burglary with which Massey (D) had been charged with was introduced. That burglary occurred in the same neighborhood and in the same month as the burglary on trial. Massey (D) contended that evidence of the second burglary was inadmissible since he had been acquitted of it in a prior trial.

ISSUE: Can evidence be introduced which relates to a crime for which the defendant has been acquitted?

HOLDING AND DECISION: Yes. An acquittal does not prevent the admissibility of evidence concerning another wrongful act, since conviction of the offense is not a prerequisite to the introduction of such evidence. Hence, the admittance of evidence of the second burglary was proper as long as it was relevant. The general tests of the admissibility of evidence in a criminal case are: is it a part of the res gestae? If not, does it tend logically, naturally, and by reasonable inference, to establish any material fact? If it does, then it is admissible whether it embraces the commission of another crime or does not and whether the other crime be similar in kind or part of a single design or not. Here, the evidence of the second burglary was pertinent to the issue of intent.

EDITOR'S ANALYSIS: As stated above evidence of another crime must be substantially relevant for some purpose other than to show a probability that the accused committed the crime on trial because he has a criminal nature.

Some of the possible "other purposes" are: to complete the story of the crime on trial by proving its immediate context; to prove the existence of a larger continuing plan or conspiracy of which the crime on trial is a part; to prove other like crimes by the defendant so nearly identical in method as to earmark them as committed by the accused, to show a passion or propensity for illicit sexual relations with the particular person concerned in the crime on trial; to show that the act on trial was not inadvertent, unintentional or without guilty knowledge; to establish motive; to show, by immediate inference, malice, deliberation, ill will, or the specific intent required for the crime on trial; to prove identity; and to impeach the accused when he takes the stand as a witness.

OLIPHANT v KOEHLER

594 F.2d 547 (6th Cir. 1979)

NATURE OF CASE: Appeal from denial of writ of habeas corpus.

FACT SUMMARY: Oliphant (D) successfully used the same methods of making a rape appear to be consensual for two rapes, but was convicted for a third rape after the first two victims testified about his methods in the third trial.

CONCISE RULE OF LAW: Testimony of previous victims of the same crime by the same defendant is admissible to show similar acts within later crimes and is not barred by double jeopardy prohibitions or collateral estoppel even though the defendant was acquitted of the earlier crimes.

FACTS: Oliphant (D) used certain methods to avoid any appearance of the use of any force or threats when committing a rape in order to make the act appear consensual. Oliphant (D) successfully avoided conviction in two previous rapes using the same methods and claiming that the victim had consented as his defense. In the trial for the rape of a third victim, the government presented the two previous victims as rebuttal witnesses. The testimony of these witnesses was used to prove that Oliphant (D) intended to force his victims to have intercourse by purposely using the same methods each time. Oliphant (D) appealed on the grounds that he was being subjected to double jeopardy by this rebuttal testimony and that it was a relitigation of the same issue (of whether or not the first two victims consented) which is barred by collateral estopel.

ISSUE: May previous victims testify of previous closely similar crimes to rebut a defendant's denial of intention in a later crime even though defendant was acquitted of the previous crime?

HOLDING AND DECISION: (J. Weick) Yes. Oliphant's (D) two previous rape victims may testify to show Oliphant's repeated use of his methods of coercion in order to show that Oliphant (D) intended and fully orchestrated the events allowing him to commit rape without threats of bodlly harm. Consent to intercourse in such identically undersirable situations becomes very difficult to believe when it occurs for the third time in a row. But since each victim's decision to give or withold consent was a different issue, each rape was not part of the same episode nor did they turn on a common crucial fact. Oliphant (D) is being tried only on the issue of his intention to rape the third victim and not on his intent to rape the first two victims.

DISSENT: (C. J. Edwards) The rebuttal testimony forces a jury to reconsider whether or not Oliphant (D) also intended to rape the first two victims in order to decide whether Oliphant (D) used an ongoing scheme to compel the third victim to have intercourse. This reconsideration of intention is double jeopardy.

EDITOR'S ANALYSIS: Evidence of past similar acts cannot be used to show a characteristic propensity for a defendant to commit a crime. Such evidence can be used to rebut a defendant's denial of any intention to do certain acts by showing that the defendant did the same acts repeatedly in the past. Often the only reliable evidence of such past acts is evidence from past trials for the same crime. While there is great risk that a jury may wish to convict a defendant who appears to have mistakenly escaped punishment before, and thereby subject the defendant to double jeopardy, the disallowance of such evidence may reward criminals for schemes which successfully mitigate incriminating evidence and allow the repitition of "safe" crimes.

NOTES:

MICHELSON v. UNITED STATES

SUPREME COURT OF THE UNITED STATES,
1948. 335 U.S. 469, 69 S. Ct. 213

NATURE OF CASE: Prosecution for the bribery of a federal revenue agent.

FACT SUMMARY: While admitting he was guilty of giving money to the federal officer, Michelson (D) claimed that it was done in response to the agent's threats, demands and solicitation.

CONCISE RULE OF LAW: Where a defendant introduces evidence of his good character/reputation in the community, the prosecution may cross-examine these character witness about events or crimes, in defendant's past, which would tend to adversely affect defendant's reputation.

FACTS: At trial, Michelson (D) claimed entrapment. He stated that the federal officer had threatened, demanded and solicited the bribe Michelson (D) had given him. Michelson (D) called five witnesses to testify as to his good character/reputation in the community. All were asked by the prosecution if they had heard that Michelson (D) had been arrested for receiving stolen goods 27 years ago. On direct, Michelson (D) had mentioned that he had once been arrested about 20 years before. The judge scrupulously instructed the jury to disregard the actual event and view the comment as merely testing the witness's standard of opinion as to Michelson's (D) reputation. The judge, before the prosecution was allowed to even ask this question, met with both sides and ascertained that this was an actual event which would probably result in some comment among acquaintances, if not injury, to Michelson's (D) reputation. Michelson (D) was convicted and appeals from the trial judge's allowance of this cross-examination.

ISSUE: May the prosecution question character witnesses concerning past events or crimes which would tend to damage defendant's reputation?

HOLDING AND DECISION: Yes. The law in this area is purely decisional. It is archaic and illogical, yet so widespread that we must weigh the value of an almost imperceptible logical advancement in the law against the confusion and error it would engender. The policy of the law is to exclude testimony concerning a person's past reputation or crimes. This is not because the evidence has no probative value, but because of the prejudice it does to the defendant. The likelihood of the jury giving too great a weight to this testimony outweighs the inferences provided by the evidence. However, no such restrictions are placed on the defendant in a criminal prosecution. He may, as Michelson (D) did, call various witnesses to testify as to his general character. General character is synonymous with reputation. The witness must establish that he knows the defendant and is a member of the community in which the defendant resides. Testimony as to specific acts or conduct is not permitted. The witness may only testify as to hearsay concerning the community's perception of defendant's reputation. This tends to help establish defendant as a person incapable of committing the crime charged and may even be sufficient, in certain circumstances, to be so favorable as to raise a reasonable doubt of guilt. Edgington v. United States, 164 U.S. 361, 17 S.Ct. 72, 41 L.Ed. 467. A jury, in Federal Court, may be so instructed if the case warrants it. However, once defendant opens the door, his witnesses may be cross-examined as to acts which, if they were aware of them, might tend to damage defendant's character in the community. Further, they may shed light on factors the witnesses have used to form their opinion and on how well they really know the defendant. "The witness must qualify to give an opinion by showing such acquaintance with the defendant, the community in which he has lived, and the circle in which he has moved, as to speak with authority of the terms in which he is regarded." While, generally speaking, the assumption is that if no ill is reported, defendant's reputation must be good, it is only viable if the witness has had access to said information. Michelson (D) was arrested 27 years before the current conviction. Several of his witnesses testified that they had known him for 30 years. While rehabilitation may have occurred, the question at issue is how Michelson's (D) community receives him. An arrest without conviction may be as damaging to a reputation as a conviction. The fact that the crimes are not similar is irrelevant as the issue is general character. The trial judge should be given great latitude in allowing or excluding this type of cross-examination. Being there, observing the witnesses, makes him a far more competent party to determine this matter. While this is an illogical paradoxical situation (admitting evidence that would not be normally admissible), the judge's jury instructions and warnings are alleged to be adequate protection. This is admittedly a rather fallacious assumption, but the substitution of a new rule prohibiting this type of cross-examination (followed by only one State) would lead to far greater difficulties. Judgment affirmed.

EDITOR'S ANALYSIS: The general rule that a witness may only testify as to a defendant's reputation in the community has been somewhat changed by the holding in United States v. Parker, 447 F. 2d 826 (7th Circuit 1971). There, the court held that a character witness could testify concerning defendant's reputation among his co-workers. Generally speaking, character evidence is introduced to bolster defendants' protestations of innocence. The testimony is supposed to establish that defendant lacks the criminal propensities necessary to having committed the crime. A good reputation tends to show that defendant has not been in trouble, either legally or morally. Therefore, specific acts, conduct or the witness's own opinion are irrelevant. It is the way that the community views the defendant which is to be established. Rationally, most character witnesses will be testifying as to how they view the defendant.

HESS v. MARINARI

81 W. Va. 500, 94S. E. 968 (1918)

NATURE OF CASE: Appeal from award of damages for assault.

FACT SUMMARY: Marinari (D), who threatened a violent crowd with a meat cleaver, allegedly striking Hess (P) in an attempt to clear the crowd out of his store, claimed that Hess (P) received his wounds in a street brawl outside and that damages awarded to Hess (P) were excessive.

CONCISE RULE OF LAW: When it is necessary for a plaintiff to prove facts and intent constituting a crime to win damages in a civil suit, defendant's character evidence is admissable to negate the possibility of criminal intent and thereby diminish the justification for punitive damages.

FACTS: Marinari (D) owned and operated a general store. A crowd of men began arguing violently inside of his store. Hess (P) walked over to see what was causing the disturbance. Marinari (D), fearing damage to his store, brandished a meat cleaver and ordered everyone to leave his store. Hess (P) claimed that Marinari (D) went further than this by striking at people with the cleaver to drive them out and struck Hess (P) on the shoulder. Marinari (D) claimed that Hess (P) sustained his injuries in the brawl occurring in the street immediately after the crowd exited his store. The trial court refused to allow Marinari (D) to present evidence of his generally non-violent character to counter Hess'(P) claim of intentional injury. Marinari (D) appealed the $9,000 damages awarded Hess (P) by the jury.

ISSUE: May a defendant present evidence of his good character in a civil suit if the plaintiff must prove facts sufficient to support criminal intent in order to be awarded punitive damages?

HOLDING AND DECISION: (J. Ritz) Yes. Since a defendant may present evidence of good character to deny criminal intent in a criminal trial, there is no reason why a defendant in a civil trial cannot do the same when intent is an issue in the allegation of an intentional tort. Punitive damages are meant to punish, just as fines and imprisonment are intended to punish a person for violating the criminal law. No one should be punished in a purely punitive fashion without the requisite intent being proven. Nor should anyone be denied an opportunity to refute intent with evidence of good character.

EDITOR'S ANALYSIS: In a suit for damages alleging an intentional tort, compensatory damages must be distinguished from punitive damages. Intent needs to be shown only to sustain punitive damages, not compensatory damages. Thus while character evidence is admissable when punitive damages are to be awarded, it is not admissible when only compensatory damages are considered.

MUTUAL LIFE INS. CO. v. KELLY

Ct. of Appls. of Ohio, 1934, 49 Ohio App. 319, 197 N.E.235

NATURE OF CASE: Appeal from an award of damages upon an insurance policy.

FACT SUMMARY: Mutual (D) claimed that it was error for Kelly (P), who sued for the proceeds of a life insurance policy upon which Mutual (D) refused to pay, to introduce evidence of the deceased insured's good character.

CONCISE RULE OF LAW: In civil actions, even where fraud is imputed or dishonesty is charged, evidence of a party's good or bad character is incompetent in evidence unless it is made an issue by the pleadings or the proof.

FACTS: Farson, the decedent, had a life insurance policy issued by Mutual (D) with Kelly (P) named as the beneficiary. Farson died when fatally injured by a spring gun inside a vacant cottage. Kelly (P) sued Mutual (D) who refused to pay the proceeds of the policy. The policy was conditioned so that Mutual (D) was not required to pay when the insured died in consequence of his own criminal action or from his violation of the law. Farson and a companion had purchased a pair of pliers before going mushroom hunting. They came upon a locked cottage. Apparently using the pliers, Farson opened a screen door and was shot by a spring gun when he opened the front door. At trial, no evidence was introduced to show that Farson had ever done a prior similar act. Only facts and circumstances pertaining to the incident were introduced. In rebuttal, Kelly (P) brought forth witnesses who testified as to Farson's good reputation and peaceable, law-abiding nature. Kelly (P) received judgment and Mutual (D) appealed claiming that the rebuttal testimony was erroneously admitted.

ISSUE: In civil actions, even where fraud is imputed or dishonesty is charged, is evidence of a party's good or bad character incompetent in evidence unless it is made an issue by the pleadings or the proof?

HOLDING AND DECISION: Yes. In civil actions, even where fraud is imputed or dishonesty is charged, evidence of a party's good or bad character is incompetent in evidence unless it is made an issue by the pleadings or the proof. This is unlike in a criminal action where such evidence is allowed. Here, the action is upon a contract wherein the insured's general character was not involved. Such evidence is a matter of opinion and can only delay litigation and increase expenses. The party's good reputation is presumed until either attacked by the pleading or the proof. Thus, evidence of Farson's good character, being presumed, was surplusage and prejudicial. Such evidence apparently led the jury to believe that the decedent's trespass was a merely technical one when all other evidence showed it to be criminal. Reversed and new trial ordered.

EDITOR'S ANALYSIS: As a general rule, character evidence is not admissible in civil cases with a few exceptions. Those exceptions are cases where character would be necessarily in issue such as actions for libel and slander, malicious prosecution and seduction. Otherwise, such evidence is thought to have little probative value and is outweighed by it's potential prejudice.

PHINNEY v. DETROIT UNITED RAILWAY CO.

232 Mich. 399, 205 N.W. 124 (1925)

NATURE OF CASE: Appeal on a writ of error of judgment for defendant.

FACT SUMMARY: A motorman, employed by Detroit United (D), failed to use all possible methods for stopping a train and collided into a car crossing the track, killing Phinney's (P) wife, but could not be shown to be negligent because the court refused to admit character evidence of the motorman's reputation for recklessness.

CONCISE RULE OF LAW: Character evidence in the form of reputation is inadmissible in a civil suit for compensatory damages alleging negligence.

FACTS: Detroit United's (D) motorman saw the car carrying Phinney's (D) wife as a passenger approach the railroad track crossing. Thinking that the car would stop, the motorman failed to apply the brakes until the train was 40 feet from the crossing. The motorman also failed to use the most effective method to stop the train. Phinney (P) was not allowed to introduce evidence of the motorman's reputation for recklessness known by other Detroit United (D) employees. Because the motorman made a reasonable effort to stop the train, Phinney (P) received no damages for his wife's death in the collision. Phinney (P) appealed.

ISSUE: May character evidence in the form of reputation be introduced to prove a propensity for an individual to act negligently in a specific situation?

HOLDING AND DECISION: (J. Ritz) No. Character evidence in the form of a reputation may not be used to prove that a person acted negligently. Regardless of what degree of recklessness Detroit United's (D) motorman operated trains in the past, the court is concerned only with the operation of the train in this particular incident. If the motorman made a reasonably prudent attempt to avoid the collision, but still failed to do so, the mere possibiltiy of more effective means will not be sufficient to prove negligence within an emergency situation. Reputation based on past acts is irrelevant to whether the motorman's actions prior to this accident were in fact negligent.

EDITOR'S ANALYSIS: Intent is not an issue in this case. Character evidence to show a propensity to act in a certain way can only go to show an intention. It cannot show that certain acts did in fact occur. Rather than punishing the defendant for a reputation, the court sought to impose a minimal standard of conduct by which to judge the defendant's actions in one particular incident.

DALLAS RAILWAY AND TERMINAL CO. v. FARNSWORTH

148 Tex. 584, 227 S.W.2d 1017 (1950)

NATURE OF CASE: Appeal from award of damages for negligence.

FACT SUMMARY: Farnsworth (P) testified about Dallas Co.'s (D) streetcar driver hurrying through stops throughout her ride prior to hitting her with the streetcar when the driver failed to wait until she had stepped away from the streetcar before taking off.

CONCISE RULE OF LAW: Character evidence of reputation of past acts is admissible to show negligence only if the evidence is connected to the facts at issue in some special way beyond mere similarity.

FACTS: Farnsworth (P) observed the Dallas Co. (D) streetcar driver barely allow time for passengers to step off the streetcar, and failed to see if they were clear before taking off at three stops prior to the stop at which she got off. The streetcar resumed its momentum just as Farnsworth (P) stepped onto the pavement after being the last passenger to exit from the rear. The rear end of the street car struck Farnsworth (P) as it swung out from the track while the streetcar turned. Farnsworth (P) testified about the driver's hurried previous stops to show that the driver was negligently hurried at her stop as well. Dallas Co. (P) appealed.

ISSUE: May character evidence of past acts be used to demonstrate negligence in a later act if the past acts and the later act at issue are connected in a special way beyond mere similarity?

HOLDING AND DECISION: Yes. Normally, character evidence in either the form of reputation or past acts cannot be used to prove negligence because their only connection to the facts at issue are limited similarities. But in this case, the Dallas Co. (P) driver can be shown to be in a hurry at the time of the accident by showing that he was in a hurry immediately prior to the accident. The driver's past acts are not only similar but directly connected to his acts at the time of the accident.

EDITOR'S ANALYSIS: This exception to the rule against admitting character evidence to prove negligence is very limited. It is not altogether clear whether the driver's past hurried acts were indeed past acts or actually part of the event resulting in the accident.

NOTES:

CLARK v. STEWART

126 Ohio St. 263, 185 N.E.71 (1933)

NATURE OF CASE: Appeal of personal injury case.

FACT SUMMARY: Clark (P) cross-examined (D) about past acts of reckless driving committed by his minor son who had inflicted injury upon Clark (P) while driving his father's, Stewart's, (D) car.

CONCISE RULE OF LAW: Not included in casebook excerpt.

FACTS: Stewart's (D) son was an inexperienced 17-year-old driver. Stewart (D) nonetheless employed his son to drive Stewart's (D) car to deliver things for him. While on such an errand, Stewart's (D) son hit Clark (P) and injured him. Clark (P) sought to introduce past acts of reckless driving committed by Stewart's (D) son to show that Stewart's (D) son was an incompetant driver, whom Stewart (D) negligently permitted to drive his car, by cross-examining Stewart (D) about his son's past accidents. Stewart (D) appealed.

ISSUE: Not included in casebook excerpt.

HOLDING AND DECISION: (J. Stephenson) Not included in casebook excerpt.

EDITOR'S ANALYSIS: The excerpt from the cross examination is a good illustration of the inadmissable introduction of character evidence to prove negligence if the cross examination were used solely to introduce character evidence. In the actual case cited above, the allowance of this cross examination was affirmed because it was use to show that Stewart (D) had knowledge of his sons's incompetance, yet still permitted his son to drive his car. This knowledge, in addition to respondeat superior liability, made Stewart (D) liable for any negligence proven to be committed by his son. This excerpt is also a good example of how to have inadmissible character evidence admitted into the record by using another basis for admission.

NOTES:

MEYER v. UNITED STATES

464 F. Supp. 317 (D. Colo. 1979)

NATURE OF CASE: Action for damages for personal injury.

FACT SUMMARY: Meyer (P) sought to recover for damages for personal injury resulting from dental surgery involving the extraction of wisdom teeth.

CONCISE RULE OF LAW: Evidence of habit, one's regular response to a repeated specific situation, is admissible to show that a person acted in conformity with the habit when confronted with a particular situation.

FACTS: After examination by Dr. Aitkin, Meyer (P) was advised that extraction of her wisdom teeth was recommended, since they were impacted. Two weeks later, Meyer (P) returned, and the wisdom teeth were extracted. Shortly thereafter, she started experiencing slight right side numbness, loss of sensation, and loss of taste. It was agreed that she has suffered lingual nerve damage. Dr. Aitkin was experienced in the extraction of wisdom teeth. Meyer (P) filed suit following the earlier filing of an administrative claim. Aitkin testified to the procedures that he followed in this case, and on the issue of informed consent, stating that his habit and custom was to give standard advice to patients about the extraction of wisdom teeth including a warning about the potential for nerve damage. Testimony of two dental assistants supported the contention of Dr. Aitkin that he regularly and routinely advised patients as to the risks involved in the extraction of wisdom teeth. Meyer (P) testified that she received no warning or advice.

ISSUE: Is evidence of habit, one's regular response to a repeated specific situation, admissible to show that a person acted in conformity with the habit when confronted by the specific situation?

HOLDING AND DECISION: (Finesilver, J.) Yes. Evidence of habit, one's regular response to a repeated specific situation, is admissible to show that a person acted in conformity with the habit when confronted with the specific situation. Habit can be characterized as a person's practice of handling a specific type of situation with a particular type of conduct, it is a person's usual way of acting, a custom or practice. Even though the actual giving of advice and warning was in question, there was substantial evidence that Dr. Aitkin routinely and regularly informed patients of the procedures and the risks involved in the extraction of widsom teeth, and therefore was in compliance with the local laws requiring informed consent as to the procedures and risks involved in surgical operations. Judgment for Aitken (D).

EDITOR'S ANALYSIS: Note that the courts in admitting evidence of habit to show that a person acted in conformity with the habit in a given situation employ a very narrow definition of habit. Habit must be distinguished from character. Character is a generalized description of a person's disposition in respect to a general trait (McCormick on Evidence, 3rd Ed., pg. 574.) Evidence of character is generally held to be of less probative value that is evidence of habit, and usually contains a greater prejudicial value as well.

UNITED STATES v. BEECHUM

U.S. Ct. of Appls., 5th Cir.,1978. 582 F. 2d 898

NATURE OF CASE: Appeal from a conviction for mail theft.

FACT SUMMARY: To establish that substitute letter carrier Beechum (D) had intentionally and unlawfully possessed a silver dollar taken from the mails, the United States (P) introduced evidence that he possessed two credit cards not belonging to him and which had been sent through the mails.

CONCISE RULE OF LAW: Under the Federal Rules, evidence that the defendant committed other crimes is admissible to prove intent if it possesses probative value that is not substantially outweighed by its undue prejudice.

FACTS: Beechum (D), a substitute letter carrier, was convicted of unlawfully possessing an 1890 silver dollar which he knew to be stolen from the mails, in violation of 18 USCA Section 1708. On appeal, he challenged the admission at his trial of evidence that two Sears, Roebuck & Co. credit cards were found in his wallet when he was arrested. The cards, which had been issued to persons other than Beechum (D), had been sent through the mails 10 months earlier and were as yet unsigned. The evidence was admitted as proof of Beechum's (D) criminal intent in keeping the silver dollar. The panel which first heard the appeal was of the opinion that the Broadway case still covered such a situation and had survived intact the passage of the Federal Rules of Civil Procedure. Broadway and its progeny required that the essential physical elements of the extrinsic offense include those of the offense charged and that each of these elements be proved by plain, clear, and convincing evidence before an extrinsic offense could be introduced on the issue of criminal intent.

ISSUE: Is evidence of intrinsic offenses admissible to show criminal intent if it possesses probative value that is not substantially outweighed by its undue prejudice?

HOLDING AND DECISION: (J. Tjoflat) Yes. Broadway's requirements did not survive the enactment of the Federal Rules, which permit introduction of evidence of other crimes committed by a defendant (to show criminal intent) if such possesses probative value which is not substantially outweighed by its undue prejudice. It is only when such evidence is offered to prove a defendant's character that its probative value is automatically outweighed by its undue prejudice. In this case, the extrinsic offense evidence is offered to show intent, the extrinsic offense and the charged offense involve the same state of mind (intent), and the evidence would be sufficient for a jury to find Beechum (D) committed the extrinsic offenses. Under such circumstances, the judge did not abuse his discretion in finding the probative value of the extrinsic offense evidence was not substantially outweighed by undue prejudice. Affirmed.

DISSENT: (J. Goldberg) Broadway and its doctrines remain sound, as evidenced by the fact that many circuits have preserved similar doctrines in the wake of the passage of the Federal Rules. Furthermore, the test the majority embraces to replace Broadway is much more subjective in nature and even more hostile to extrinsic offense evidence than Broadway in some respects.

EDITOR'S ANALYSIS: Unlike this case, there are many instances where a judge will not know at the commencement of the trial if the issue of intent will be contested. Thus, he is in a poor position to weigh the probative value of extrinsic offense evidence against its undue prejudice. This case refused to address the issue of whether or not a mere plea of not guilty can justify the government's introduction of such evidence in its case in chief. When the Sixth Circuit considered the question in 1975 (United States v. Ring, 513 F. 2d 1001), it held such evidence inadmissible in the case in chief where innocent intent had not been pleaded.

NOTES:

UNITED STATES v. PAIGE

464 F. Supp. 99 (D. Pa. 1978)

NATURE OF CASE: **Motion to exclude evidence of prior conviction in possession of stolen securities case.**

FACT SUMMARY: **Paige (D) moved to prevent the government (P) from using evidence of a prior conviction to impeach his credibility at his trial for possession of stolen securities.**

CONCISE RULE OF LAW: **The use of evidence of prior conviction of a crime similar to the crime charged for purposes of impeachment is highly prejudicial, and such evidence is generally not admissible unless strong justification is shown.**

FACTS: Paige (D) pleaded guilty in 1970 to possession of stolen goods. Eight years later, he was charged with the knowing receipt of stolen securities. During the eight-year interim, Paige (D) had not been convicted of any other crimes. Paige moved to prevent the government (P) from impeaching his credibility with the use of the prior conviction.

ISSUE: Is the use of evidence of prior conviction of a crime similar to the crime charged for purposes of impeachment so highly prejudicial that the evidence will be generally excluded unless strong justification is shown?

HOLDING AND DECISION: (Newcomer, J.) Yes. The use of evidence of prior conviction of a crime similar to the crime charged is highly prejudicial, and such evidence is generally not admissible unless strong justification is shown. The prosecution can attack the credibility of a witness through the use of prior convictions punishable by imprisonment in excess of one year if it can show that the probative value of a prior conviction's use outweighs its prejudicial effect. Among the factors to be considered in this process of balancing are the point in time of the previous conviction and the witness's subsequent history, the similarity between the past crime and the charged crime, and the importance of the witness's testimony. In this case, the government did not meet its burden of proof. While the prior conviction reflects adversely on Paige's (D) honesty and integrity, its probative value was diminished by his clean record for eight years following the prior conviction. Case law seems clear that when the past crime and the crime charged are similar, as here, failure to exclude such evidence is highly prejudicial. Paige's (D) testimony here was crucial in order to rebut the inference of guilt that would have arisen if he had failed to explain the possession of stolen securities to the satisfaction of the jury. Justice requires that unless strong justification is shown by the government (P), use of the prior conviction should not be allowed. Motion granted.

EDITOR'S ANALYSIS: Questions as to the proper use of prior convictions for the purpose of impeachment usually arise only when there is an attempt to impeach a criminal defendant. In civil cases, or to impeach prosecution witnesses, the use of prior convictions to impeach is unlimited, and there is no requirement to balance the prejudicial and probative values of the evidence.

UNITED STATES v. FEARWELL

595 F. 2d 771 (D.C. Circuit, 1979)

NATURE OF CASE: **Appeal from conviction for conspiracy to violate the Food Stamp Act.**

FACT SUMMARY: **After Fearwell (D) declined to testify at trial, he was convicted of conspiracy to violate the Food Stamp Act.**

CONCISE RULE OF LAW: **Evidence of a prior conviction for petit larceny may not be admitted for the purpose of attacking the credibility of a witness.**

FACTS: Fearwell (D) was convicted of conspiracy to violate the Food Stamp Act. Prior to trial, the prosecution (P) informed defense counsel that if Fearwell (D) chose to testify, it intended to impeach his credibility by introducing evidence of his prior conviction of attempted petit larceny, and the trial court ruled that it would permit the prosecution to proceed with the impeachment as planned. On appeal, Fearwell (D) argued that the crime of petit larceny was not a crime which must be admitted pursuant to Federal Rule of Evidence 609(a)(2). That provision stipulates that for impeachment purposes, "evidence that (a witness) has been convicted shall be admitted . . . but only if the crime . . . (2) involved dishonesty or false statement, regardless of the punishment."

ISSUE: May evidence of a prior conviction for petit larceny be admitted for the purpose of attacking the credibility of a witness?

HOLDING AND DECISION: (C. J. Skelly Wright) No. Evidence of a prior conviction for petit larceny may not be admitted for the purpose of attacking the credibility of a witness. Under Rule 609(a)(2), the trial judge must permit the use of the prior conviction for impeachment purposes if the crime underlying the conviction involved dishonesty or false statement. The crime of petit larceny is not one characterized by an element of deceit or deliberate interference with a court's ascertainment of truth. Thus, it is not a crime involving dishonesty or false statement. Rule 609(a)(2) must be confined to a narrow subset of crimes that bear directly upon the accused's propensity to testify truthfully. The present case is thus remanded.

EDITOR'S ANALYSIS: The Conference Report to Federal Rule 609(a)(2) discusses the types of crimes involving dishonesty and false statement. "By the phrase 'dishonesty and false statement' the Conference means crimes such as perjury or subornation of perjury, false statement, criminal fraud, embezzlement, or false pretense, or any other offense in the nature of crimen falsi, the commission of which involves some element of deceit, untruthfulness, or falsification bearing on the accused's propensity to testify truthfully."

NOTES:

UNITED STATES v. SIMS

588 F.2d 1145 (1978)

NATURE OF CASE: Appeal from conviction for possession of a firearm as a previously convicted felon.

FACT SUMMARY: Sims (D) appealed his conviction for possession of a firearm as a previously convicted felon, claiming reversible error in the government's (P) use of two prior convictions, both of which were over 10-years-old, to impeach Sims (D).

CONCISE RULE OF LAW: It is reversible error to allow the use of prior convictions for the purpose of impeachment where the convictions are over 10-years-old and their probative value does not substantially outweigh their prejudicial effect.

FACTS: In 1977, Sims (D) was arrested while driving his car. A search of the car turned up a gun which had been previously stolen from the home of one of Sims' (D) neighbors. Sims (D) was charged with being a convicted felon in the possession of a firearm. The underlying felony used in the indictment was Sims' (D) prior conviction in 1970 for possession of stolen property. Sims (D) denied any knowledge of the gun being in his car until it was found. The first trial on this indictment ended in a jury deadlock. At the second trial, the prosecution introduced for purposes of impeachment evidence of a 21-year-old conviction for burglary and a 12-year-old conviction for interstate transportation of a stolen motor vehicle. Sims (D) was convicted and appealed.

ISSUE: Is it reversible error to allow the use of prior convictions for the purpose of impeachment where the convictions are over 10-years-old and the probative value of their use does not substantially outweigh their prejudicial effect?

HOLDING AND DECISION: (Phillips, C.J.) Yes. It is reversible error to allow the use of prior convictions for the purpose of impeachment where the convictions are over 10-years-old and their probative value does not substantially outweigh their prejudicial effect. In order for a conviction more than 10-years-old to be used for impeachment purposes, the trial judge must make this determination after examining the facts and circumstances surrounding the particular case in question. The purpose behind the rule is to prevent conviction as a result of the prejudicial, cumulative effect of an old criminal record. Old convictions normally have little probative value on the tendency of a witness towards truthfulness or veracity. In effect, the rule creates a rebuttable presumption that convictions over 10-years-old are more prejudicial than probative and should be excluded. The court cannot allow the inference to arise that it is more likely that a defendant committed the offense for which he is being tried because he has committed crimes in the past. In this case, Sims (D) credibility, in that he claimed that he had no knowledge of the gun, was essentially the entire case. Given the relatively weak probative value of stale convictions, and the desire to prevent conviction of a defendant on the basis of an old prior criminal record, it is clear that the obvious prejudice resulting from the admission of the two old convictions clearly outweighed their probative value on the credibility issue. It would be contrary to the purpose of the rule to allow the government (P), after a previous mistrial, to bolster its case with the use of stale convictions. The trial court abused its discretion in allowing the use of the two old convictions. Reversed; remanded for new trial.

DISSENT: (Engel, J.) It is not clear that the trial court abused its discretion in allowing the use of the two old convictions for the purpose of impeachment. The prejudicial effect is considerably lessened in this case by the nature of the crime charged; the jury was already aware of Sims' (D) record. Where credibility is an essential issue, the jury should be allowed as much information as possible to help in the determination of the issue.

EDITOR'S ANALYSIS: Federal Rule of Evidence 609(b) embodies the rule followed in this case. Note that the general rule with respect to the use of prior convictions for purposes of impeachment is altered in several substantive ways, most notably that the balancing test that is applied also goes to crimes involving dishonesty or false statement, and the probative value must substantially outweigh the prejudicial effect.

NOTES:

UNITED STATES v. PISARI

636 F.2d 855 (1981)

NATURE OF CASE: Reconsideration of reversal of conviction for robbery.

FACT SUMMARY: The court reconsidered its earlier opinion reversing Pisari's (D) conviction for robbery of a postal installation, in which it held rebuttal testimony of Coombs, a government (P) witness, was improperly admitted.

CONCISE RULE OF LAW: Extrinsic evidence which addresses itself only to a collateral matter is generally inadmissible as evidence of impeachment.

FACTS: Pisari(D) was charged with the robbery of a postal installation. At trial, Pisari (D) denied having ever engaged in robbery by knife, and the court allowed Coombs, a goverment (P) agent, to testify that Pisari (D) had told him that he had previously engaged in the robbery of a drug dealer using a knife, for impeachment purposes. The court admitted the evidence as proof of a prior inconsistent statement relevant to Pisari's (D) credibility. Pisari (D) was convicted and appealed. The Court of Appeals reversed, holding that Coombs' testimony was neither admissible as a prior inconsistent statement for purposes of impeachment nor as independent proof of Pisari's identity. Upon petition for rehearing by the government (P), the opinion was withdrawn and reconsidered.

ISSUE: Is extrinsic evidence which addresses itself only to a collateral matter generally admissible as evidence of impeachment?

HOLDING AND DECISION: (Coffin, C.J.) No. Extrinsic evidence which addresses itself only to a collateral matter is generally inadmissible as evidence of impeachment. The common law test for collateralness was quite frequently mechanical, but the better approach would be a balancing method. Evidence which would be relevant solely because it suggests that the witness may have lied about something in the past would generally be excluded because of its low probative value and its tendency to prejudice. In the present case, the government (P), tried to avoid the collateralness issue by introducing the evidence as independent proof of Pisari's (D) identity. The only similarity in the crime described by Coombs and the crime charged was the use of a knife, and this is an insufficient "trademark" upon which to base an inference of identity. Since Coombs' testimony addressed itself only to the collateral matter of the previous robbery, it was improperly admitted as impeachment evidence. It could not be said that this error was harmless. Reversed and remanded.

EDITOR'S ANALYSIS: Facts relevant to the substantive issues of a case are clearly not collateral. Facts which would be independently provable by extrinsic evidence, such as facts that show bias, interest, etc., are also facts which are not considered collateral. The federal courts embrace the balancing method used in the present case.

NOTES:

COMMONWEALTH v. GOUVEIA

371 Mass. 566, 358 N.E. 2d 1001 (1876)

NATURE OF CASE: **Appeal from conviction for rape.**

FACT SUMMARY: **Gouveia (D) appealed from his conviction for rape and for committing an unnatural act, claiming the trial court erred in excluding evidence of prior sexual intercourse of the victim with persons other than Gouveia (D).**

CONCISE RULE OF LAW: **The general rule that in rape cases evidence of instances of prior sexual intercourse of the victim with persons other than the defendant is inadmissible is not limited solely to those cases where consideration of these issues would tend to prolong a trial or confuse the issues.**

FACTS: The victim drove to a local bar and had a few drinks with friends and with a man (not Gouveia (D)) who invited her to a party. She drove him and went with him to the party. A half hour after they arrived, they returned to her car, where she got ill, and he passed out. After a time, she noticed that her wallet and car keys were missing. She left the car, and Gouveia (D) suggested that she could lie down in his van, which she did. Several men looked in on her, and one man made sexual advances towards her, which she repulsed. Gouveia (D) then allegedly entered the van and committed the crimes charged. She left the van and returned to the car. Gouveia (D) later gave her a ride home, lying about the location of the party and the ownership of the van. She noted the license plate of the van when Gouveia (D) drove off. Gouveia (D) was charged with rape and committing an unnatural act. The victim's original escort and seven of his relatives testified for Gouveia (D) as to the victim's obscene behavior on the night in question, but all testimony as to prior sexual intercourse of the victim with persons other than Gouveia (D) was excluded. Gouveia (D) was convicted and appealed, where his sentence was reduced, whereupon he brought this further appeal.

ISSUE: Should the general rule in rape cases, that evidence of instances of prior sexual intercourse of the victim with persons other than the defendant is inadmissible, be limited solely to those cases where consideration of these matters would tend to prolong the trial or confuse the issue?

HOLDING AND DECISION: (Braucher, J.) No. The general rule in rape cases, that evidence of instances of sexual intercourse of the victim with persons other than the defendant is inadmissible, should not be limited to those cases where consideration of those matters would tend to prolong the trial or confuse the issues. The general rule is a reflection of the principle that a victim's consent to have intercourse with one man is not relevant to the question of whether she consented to intercourse with another. Since it is not relevant evidence, Gouveia (D) has not been denied his right to a fair trial. No reason has been advanced to justify limiting the application of the general rule. There was no error in excluding evidence of prior sexual acts between the victim and a person other than Gouveia (D). Affirmed.

EDITOR'S ANALYSIS: The rule enacted here reflects the modern trend towards limiting the use of evidence of the sexual history of the victim. The most typical embodiment of the rule is found in the Federal Rules of Evidence. Note that such evidence could have been introduced to show whether the accused "was or was not, with respect to the alleged victim, the source of the semen or the injury," under the Federal Rules.

NOTES:

PEOPLE v. SCHOLL

225 Cal. App. 2d 558, 37 Cal. Rptr. 475 (1964)

NATURE OF CASE: Appeal from order denying new trial motion in sexual assault case.

FACT SUMMARY: Scholl (D) appealed from an order of the trial court denying him a new trial after being convicted of committing sexual offenses upon a eight-year-old girl.

CONCISE RULE OF LAW: Where it is possible that the victim in a child sexual assault case has been unduly influenced into making the charge by an adult, either unintentionally or because of improper motivation, the defendant should have the right to explore the propensities and motivations of the adult.

FACTS: Scholl (D) was convicted of committing sexual offenses upon an eight-year-old girl. Although there were inconsistencies and conflicts in the victim's testimony as to times, places, and circumstances, there was sufficient evidence to support the verdict. Scholl (D) attempted to cross-examine the victim's mother as to complaints made about advances made upon her by various men. The court rejected the proffer. Four witnesses testified that the mother's reputation for truthfulness was not good. Scholl (D) made a motion for a new trial, which was denied, and he appealed from the order denying his motion.

ISSUE: Where it is possible that the victim in a child sexual assault case has been unduly influenced into making the charge by an adult, either unintentionally or because of improper motivation, should the defendant have the right to explore the propensities and motivations of the adult?

HOLDING AND DECISION: (Kingsley, J.) Yes. Where it is possible that the victim in a child sexual assault case has been unduly influenced into making the charge by an adult, the defendant should have the right to explore the propensities and motivations of the adult. In child sexual assault cases, there is frequently no corroborating evidence to support the charge, the charge will rest merely on the credibility of the child witness against the defendant's denial. If such a charge is false, the defendant's defense will necessarily be based on the ability to point this out on cross-examination. Young children are expecially suggestible. An adult relative that the child trusts is in a perfect position to provide the suggestion, either unintentionally due to concern for the child, or intentionally because of bias or improper motivation on the part of the adult. Where, as in the present case, there are inconsistencies in the victim's testimony, there was a complete lack of corroborating evidence, and the truthfulness of the mother was brought into question, justice requires that the defendant should be allowed to explore the possibility that the charge might have been created in the mind of the adult, so long as the exploration is done in a reasonable manner. Order reversed.

EDITOR'S ANALYSIS: This case is an example of what might be an emerging trend in the attempt to balance protecting the victim against the accused's right to fully defend himself. The importance of the evidence sought to be excluded, and the purpose behind the exclusionary policy will have to be examined, and in most cases some reasonable amount of protection will be afforded to both of the parties.

NOTES:

COMMONWEALTH v. BOHANNON

376 Mass. 90, 378 N.E.2d 987 (1978)

NATURE OF CASE: Appeal from conviction for rape and other related crimes.

FACT SUMMARY: Bohannon (D) appealed from his conviction for rape and other related crimes, claiming error in that the trial court refused to allow Bohannon (D) to inquire into previous unsubstantiated accusations of rape on the part of the victim.

CONCISE RULE OF LAW: Evidence of prior false allegations may be used to impeach a witness's credibility, where to exclude such evidence would have a significant impact on the result of the trial and would deny the defendant the right to fully present his defense.

FACTS: Bohannon (D) and two others picked up the complainant, who was hitch-hiking. Complainant was a mildly retarded 33-year-old woman. They drove to a sandpit where various sexual acts took place. The complainant alleged that she was raped and had been forced to commit a number of unnatural sexual acts. Bohannon (D) and the others alleged that she had consented to the acts engaged in. The complainant's testimony concerning the night in question was inconsistent and confused. Bohannon (D) sought to inquire into past accusations of rape made by the complainant, and made an offer of independent proof that the complainant had made a number of unsubstantiated and apparently false accusations of rape in the past. The trial judge did not allow the inquiry, Bohannon (D) was convicted, and he appealed.

ISSUE: Can evidence of prior false allegations be used to impeach a witness's credibility, where to exclude such evidence would have a significant impact on the result of the trial and would deny the defendant the right to fully present his defense?

HOLDING AND DECISION: (Abrams, J.) Yes. Evidence of prior false allegations may be used to impeach a witness's credibility, where to exclude such evidence would have a significant impact on the result of the trial and would deny the defendant the right to fully present his defense. Generally, evidence of prior false allegations would be excluded because of the general rule that prior bad acts may not be used to impeach a witness. But the rule should not extend to the point of excluding critical evidence on crucial issues. Here, the complainant's credibility was a key issue, as she provided the only prosecution evidence on the issue of consent. Evidence of prior false allegations is directly relevant to the issue of the complainant's credibility, and likely would have a significant impact on the issue of consent and the result of the trial. Bohannon's (D) offer of proof was based on independent, third party records that the complainant had made a number of unsubstantiated allegations of rape. The inquiry in no way sought to elicit response concerning the complainant's prior sexual activity or reputation for chastity. Denying the inquiry denied Bohannon (D) the opportunity to fully present his defense. Reversed; remanded for a new trial.

EDITOR'S ANALYSIS: Under the Federal Rules of Evidence, such an inquiry into the credibility of a witness is allowed on cross-examination, so long as the cross-examination has a good faith basis for the inquiry. The instances of misconduct need not constitute a crime, and evidence of misconduct should be admitted so long as the probative value of the evidence substantially outweighs the danger of unfair prejudice.

NOTES:

BERGER v. UNITED STATES
295 U.S. 78 (1935)

NATURE OF CASE: Appeal from conviction for conspiracy to utter counterfeit notes.

FACT SUMMARY: At Berger's (D) trial for conspiracy to utter counterfeit notes, the government (P) prosecuting attorney's conduct during cross-examination clearly overstepped the bounds of propriety and fairness that should characterize the conduct of a prosecutor, and Berger (D) appealed.

CONCISE RULE OF LAW: Even though one of the purposes of cross-examination is to challenge the credibility of witnesses, the attorney conducting the questioning should conduct himself in a decorous and proper manner, and adhere to the rules of evidence.

FACTS: At Berger's (D) trial for conspiracy to utter counterfeit notes, the prosecuting attorney during cross-examination repeatedly misstated facts, put words in the witness's mouth, misconstrued witness's statements, assumed and introduced prejudicial facts not in evidence, bullied and argued with witnesses, and otherwise conducted himself in a thoroughly and dispicable and improper manner. Some objections were made and sustained as to questions, insinuations, and misstatements made, but not enough to alter the course of conduct of the prosecutor. Berger (D) was convicted and appealed.

ISSUE: Can an attorney, while cross-examining for the purpose of challenging a witness's credibility, question the witness in any manner he feels appropriate, without adherence to the rules of evidence?

HOLDING AND DECISION: (Sutherland, J.) No. Even though one of the purposes of cross-examination is to challenge the credibility of witnesses, the attorney conducting the questioning should conduct himself in a decorous and proper manner, and adhere to the rules of evidence. When an attorney conducts cross-examination in the manner that is present here, it is not clear that the improper influence of the jury of such a cross-examination could be eliminated by the limited judicial action taken here. Stern rebuke and repressive measures were called for, and if ineffective, a mistrial should have been granted.

EDITOR'S ANALYSIS: When the purpose of cross-examination is to attack the credibility of a witness, to limit the attorney to questions relevant to the main issues of the case would be crippling. Therefore, the cross-examiner has a wide latitude in the manner in which he may question the witness, and the trial judge should have the discretion to control the scope of the cross-examination. Only where one party has been substantially prejudiced will the actions of the lower court require review.

NOTES:

MILLER v. PATE

SUPREME COURT OF THE UNITED STATES, 1967.
386 U.S. 1, 87 S. Ct. 785, 17 L.Ed. 2d 690

NATURE OF CASE: **Petition for writ of habeas corpus.**

FACT SUMMARY: **In trial where Miller (D) was charged with the sexual attack and murder of a minor, the prosecution introduced a pair of shorts found near the scene which it knew to be covered with paint, but claimed, with the aid of an expert, that the shorts were smeared with blood.**

CONCISE RULE OF LAW: **The Fourteenth Amendment cannot tolerate a State criminal conviction obtained by the knowing use of false or misleading evidence.**

FACTS: Miller (D) was tried for the brutal sexual murder of a minor. There were no eyewitnesses. An important part and link in the prosecution's circumstantial case was a pair of shorts found near the scene of the crime. The shorts were covered with a dark substance which was not readily identifiable. Throughout the course of Miller's (D) trial, the prosecutor referred to the shorts as being "blood stained." The prosecutor also introduced evidence showing that the "blood" on the shorts was of the same blood type as the victim's. An expert witness for the prosecution identified the material upon the shorts as blood. Miller (D) was convicted and petitioned for a writ of habeas corpus. In the course of the proceedings, a chemical microanalyst examined the shorts and identified the stain as paint and not blood. Although the analyst could not positively swear that the shorts had never been stained with blood, it was established that the prosecutor knew, during the trial, of the real nature of the stain. The prosecutor responded by claiming that "everybody" at the trial knew that the shorts were covered with paint.

ISSUE: Does the knowing use of false or misleading evidence by the prosecution invalidate a conviction based upon that evidence?

HOLDING AND DECISION: (Stewart) Yes. The true nature of the stain was not readily apparent as the prosecution claimed. Consistent and repeated misrepresentations were made; the whole theory relating to the exhibit rested upon a distortion of the truth. The shorts were valueless as evidence since Miller (D) would not have discarded them if they had merely been covered with paint. The court has long held that a State criminal conviction based on false evidence, knowingly used by the prosecution, violates the Fourteenth Amendment.

EDITOR'S ANALYSIS: In Mooney v. Holohan, 294 U.S. 103 (1935), the seminal case on prosecutorial use of false or misleading evidence, the State had argued that "it is only where an act or omission operates so as to deprive a defendant of notice or so as to deprive him of an opportunity to present such evidence as he has, that it can be said that due process of law has been denied." The court rejected this "narrow view of the requirement of due process." The court concluded "[due process] is [not] satisfied by mere notice and hearing if a State has contrived a conviction through the pretense of a trial which in truth is but used as a means of depriving a defendant of liberty through a deliberate deception of court and jury by the presentation of testimony known to be perjured."

NOTES:

CITY OF COLUMBUS v. CARTER

71 Ohio App. 263, 49 N.E. 2d 186 (1943)

NATURE OF CASE: Not stated in casebook excerpt.

FACT SUMMARY: The trial judge visited a winess' vantage point to see how well he could see a traffic light which the witness claimed to be red while three other witnesses claimed that it was green.

CONCISE RULE OF LAW: In some circumstances, a judge may visit a place occupied by a witness in order to determine what parts of an event the witness was able to observe.

FACTS: A City (P) fire department emergency car was speeding northward on Grant Avenue while Carter (D) was driving east on Town Street. The two cars collided in the intersection of Grant and Town. The City (P) produced three witnesses who were on a street near the intersection and testified that the City (P) emergency car had a green light. Carter's (D) witness was a patient in a hospital room overlooking the intersection and testified that the emergency car had a red light. The trial judge visited the hospital room to inspect the viewpoint of Carter's (D) witness. Because the traffic light was difficult to see from the window, the judge believed the witnesses for the City (P) rather than Carter's (D) witness and held for the City (P). Carter (D) appealed the consideration by the judge of his visit to the hospital room.

ISSUE: May a trial judge visit a witness' vantage point to determine the reliability of a witness' observations?

HOLDING AND DECISION: Not stated in casebook excerpt.

EDITOR'S ANALYSIS: The judge's visit to the hospital room is known as "taking a view." A jury may also "take a view" under court supervision so as to witness the physical locality of the event and the many factors which can affect observation. Taking a view allows a jury or a judge to see physical ranges of possibility and thereby eliminate conflicting testimony which clearly denies physical possibility.

NOTES:

DOHERTY v. PROVIDENCE JOURNAL CO.

94 R.I. 392, 181 A.2d 105 (1962)

NATURE OF CASE: Appeal from denial of motion for directed verdict in action for negligence.

FACT SUMMARY: Providence (D) appealed from a denial of its motion for a directed verdict in a slip and fall case, claiming that the jury could only speculate as to whether Providence (D) had constructive notice of the slippery condition.

CONCISE RULE OF LAW: The purpose of taking a view is to aid the trier of fact in understanding evidence, and it is not evidence in itself.

FACTS: Doherty (P), a route salesman, drove to Providence's loading platform to deliver a load of bakery products to Providence's (D) cafeteria. While returning to his truck, Doherty (P) slipped on some substance next to his truck and fell, sustaining injuries. He brought suit against Providence (D), trying his case on a theory of constuctive notice. On cross-examination, Doherty (P) testified as to his familiarity with the premises, and that he always watched where he was going, even though he never saw anything on the floor. No testimony was received on the amount of time it took Doherty (P) to make his delivery and return to his truck. Testimony was received that Providence's (D) employees were responsible for keeping oil and grease off the floor. The jury was allowed to take a view of Providence's (D) operations. When Doherty (P) rested his case, Providence (D) moved for a directed verdict, claiming that in the absence of any testimony or evidence on the time it took Doherty (P) to make his delivery, the jury was not able to make any reasonable inferences on the constructive notice issue. The judge reserved his decision, and submitted the case to the jury, which returned a verdict for Doherty (D). The judge then denied Providence's (D) motion for directed verdict, and Providence (D) appealed.

ISSUE: Can a view taken by a jury be used as a substitute for evidence?

HOLDING AND DECISION: (Powers, J.) No. The purpose of taking a view is to aid the trier of fact in understanding evidence, and it is not evidence in itself. To hold otherwise would be contrary to a long line of cases which do not allow a party to substitute a view for evidence. Here, Doherty (P) argued that since the jury took a view of Providence's (D) operations, they could reasonably infer how long it would take for Doherty (P) to make his delivery. But absent any actual evidence as to the time Doherty (P) actually took, any conclusion that the jury made would have to be highly speculative. No reasonable inferences could be made from the evidence on the issue of constructive notice. The motion for directed verdict should have been granted. Exception to denial of motion for a directed verdict sustained.

EDITOR'S ANALYSIS: This case takes what is probably the majority position that a view is not evidence. Under this position, a view is only to assist the trier of fact in understanding and evaluating the evidence. The reasons behind according views nonevidentiary status, that facts obtained by a jury at a view are impossible to discern and make appellate review impractical, could be used to deny evidentiary status to many other varieties of demonstrative evidence.

CHOUINARD v. SHAW

99 N.H. 26, 104 A.2d 522 (1954)

NATURE OF CASE: Exception to refusal to grant motion for mistrial in auto accident case.

FACT SUMMARY: At a trial by jury with a view, counsel for Shaw (D) made a measurement at the view in the presence of the jury whose attention was particularly directed to it, whereupon Chouinard (P) moved for a mistrial.

CONCISE RULE OF LAW: Measurements taken at a view which are not specifically authorized by the court are improper and can constitute sufficient grounds for setting aside a verdict given certain circumstances.

FACTS: Chouinard (P) sued Shaw (D) to recover damages resulting from an automobile accident. At the view, counsel for Shaw (D) made a measurement in the presence of the jury, and directed the jury's attention to it. Chouinard (P) moved for a mistrial, and the presiding justice went to the view site and took arguements on the motion. He decided not to grant the motion and to give the jury an instruction to disregard the measurement. Chouinard (P) then excepted to the refusal to grant the motion; the trial ended in a verdict for Shaw (D); and Chouinard (P) appealed.

ISSUE: Are measurements taken at a view which are not specifically authorized by the court improper, constituting sufficient grounds for setting aside a verdict given certain circumstances?

HOLDING AND DECISION: (Kenison, C.J.) Yes. Measurements taken at a view which are not specifically authorized by the court are improper and can constitute sufficient grounds for setting aside a verdict given certain circumstances. Information that a jury obtains from a view is evidence which it is authorized to use in reaching a verdict. The manner and extent of the view are controlled by the trial court. Thus, the jury is not authorized to get evidence generally or to observe physical facts outside the scope of the view order. Similarly, tests and demonstrations not authorized are impermissible and are generally considered to be violations of the hearsay rule. It is within the discretion of the trial court to determine whether the impropriety can be cured by a limiting instruction to the jury. Here, the measurement made by Shaw's (D) counsel was found analgous to situations where a juror takes measurements or steps off distances. Where the measurement is not in dispute, such actions by a juror, while questionable and probably improper, are usually not sufficient to warrant a new trial. In cases like this, it must be presumed that a judge's limiting instruction to disregard evidence of a measurement will be followed. There was no abuse of discretion in denying the motion for mistrial. Affirmed.

EDITOR'S ANALYSIS: While the attendance of a judge is not required at a view, usually as a matter of procedure the judge is not there. The presence of the trial judge would seem to provide the best guarantee against the occurrence of improper events or demonstrations at the view, but his presence also lends strong support to the argument that since he is present, there is no reason to restrict the jury to what is specifically in the view order. Even with the judge present, some jurisdictions hold that any unauthorized test or demonstration at a view is improper under any circumstances.

ADAMCZUK v. HOLLOWAY

338 Pa. 263, 13 A.2d 2 (1940)

NATURE OF CASE: **Appeal from denial of motion for new trial in automobile accident case.**

FACT SUMMARY: **Adamczuk (P) appealed from a denial of his motion for a new trial claiming prejudicial error in the trial court's refusal to admit into evidence a certain photograph of the accident site.**

CONCISE RULE OF LAW: **If relevant, pictorial evidence should be admitted if the witness testifying to the evidence is familiar with the subject photographed and is competent to testify that the photograph correctly represents the subject.**

FACTS: Adamczuk (P) sued Holloway (D) for injuries and property damages sustained in an automobile accident. At trial, Adamczuk (P) testified that a photo shown to him (Exhibit 3) correctly represented the conditions at the intersection where the accident had occurred, except for the time of day. On cross-examination, Adamczuk (P) revealed that he had no photographic experience, did not know who had taken the photo, and was not familiar with the conditions under which the photo was taken. Holloway's (D) objections to the photo's introduction were sustained. Two subsequent attempts to introduce the photo brought similar objections and the court, noting that Adamczuk (P) had not procured the original photographer or presented any proof as to the circumstances under which the photo was taken, sustained them. The jury returned a verdict for Holloway (D), and Adamczuk (P) moved for a new trial, which was denied. Adamczuk (P) appealed.

ISSUE: If relevant, should pictorial evidence be admitted if the witness testifying to the evidence is familiar with the subject photographed and is competant to testify that the photograph correctly represents the subject?

HOLDING AND DECISION: (Maxey, J.) Yes. If relevant, pictorial evidence should be admitted if the witness testifying to the evidence is familiar with the subject photographed and competent to testify that the photograph correctly represents the subject. The photograph must be verified to allow its admission, but the photographer need not make the verification. The verification depends on the competency of the verifying witness. So long as a witness attaches his credibility to the photograph, it should be admitted. In this case, Adamczuk (P) testified that the picture accurately represented the conditions of the intersection at the time of the accident, except for the time of day. The photograph should have been introduced into evidence.

EDITOR'S ANALYSIS: This type of verification does not lend itself well to all photographic processes. For example, certain types of scientific photographs are never "seen" by witness. Under the "silent witness" theory that has developed, verification comes from the reliability of the process from which the reproduction was produced.

SISK v. STATE

232 Md. 155, 192 A.2d 108 (1963)

NATURE OF CASE: **Appeal from conviction for obtaining money by means of false pretenses.**

FACT SUMMARY: **Sisk (D) was convicted of obtaining money by means of false pretenses for cashing a check that did not belong to him and appealed, claiming a Regiscope photograph allegedly taken of him while cashing the check was improperly introduced into evidence.**

CONCISE RULE OF LAW: **The trial judge's discretion in determining the admissibility of photographic evidence does not come into play until there is competent, extrinsic evidence that the photograph is a fair representation of the subject it is supposed to represent.**

FACTS: Sisk (D) was charged with obtaining money by false pretenses for cashing a check that did not belong to him. Straver, an investigator for the store where the check was cashed, testified the check in question was endorsed by a "Charles A. Neubert, Jr.," and that when a check is cashed, a Regiscope machine numbers the check and simultaneously takes pictures of the check, the check cashier's identification and the check casher by means of a two lens camera. Straver was not present at the times the photograph was taken or developed and could not testify that the pictures were a correct likeness of what was in front of the camera when the picture was taken. Sisk (D) admitted the person in the picture was him, but denied cashing the check. The picture, practically the only evidence against Sisk (D), was admitted. Sisk (D) was convicted and appealed.

ISSUE: Does the trial judge's discretion in determining the admissibility of photographic evidence come into play if there is no competent, extrinsic evidence that the photograph is a fair representation of the subject it is supposed to represent?

HOLDING AND DECISION: (Prescott, J.) No. The trial judge's discretion in determining the admissibility of photographic evidence does not come into play until there is competent, extrinsic evidence that the photograph is a fair representation of the subject it is supposed to represent. Absent this verifying evidence, the trial judge is required to exclude the evidence. Even though Regiscope photographs are more complicated, there is no reason that the general rules governing the admissibility of photographic evidence should not apply to them. In this case, even if we take Sisk's (D) "admission" as verification for the top half of the Regiscope photograph, there was no verification of that portion of the picture representing the check and the identification used in cashing the check, and therefore, the trial judge should have excluded the Regiscope photograph. Reversed and remanded for new trial.

EDITOR'S ANALYSIS: Regiscope photographs, and other early developments in photography created some problems for the courts with respect to verification, but since they were still basicly pictures of objects "seen" by a witness, the general rules governing admissibility still applied to recent developments (i.e., colorphotographs, enlargements). Verification by the reliability of the scientific process involved developed as photography as a science developed.

STATE v. TATUM

360 P.2d 754 (Wash. 1961)

NATURE OF CASE: Appeal from conviction for forgery.

NOTES:

FACT SUMMARY: Tatum (D) was convicted of forgery in connection with the improper cashing of a welfare check and appealed, challenging the admissibility into evidence of a Regiscope photograph implicating him in the crime.

CONCISE RULE OF LAW: In order to authenticate pictorial evidence sufficiently to make it admissible, a witness need only give an indication as to when, where, and under what circumstances the photograph was taken, and that the photograph accurately portrays the subject illustrated.

FACTS: Tousin, a tenant of the same rooming house where Tatum (D) resided, did not receive his monthly welfare check. The check was later cashed at a food store. Pentecost, an employee at the food store, testified that when a check was presented to her for payment, she would initial it and insert it into a Regiscope machine, which is designed to simultaneously photograph both the check and the person cashing it. Pentecost further testified that the initials on the check in question were hers. When the endorsement on the check was discovered to be forged, the film was developed, and showed both the check and Tatum (D). Pentecost testified that the background of the picture was that of the food store, and one Dale testified as the Regiscope process. The picture was admitted, Tatum (D) was convicted, and he appealed.

ISSUE: Does authentication of pictorial evidence for admissibility require more than some indication as to when, where, and under what circumstances the photograph was taken, and that the photograph accurately portrays the subject illustrated?

HOLDING AND DECISION: (Donworth, J.) No. In order to sufficiently authenticate pictorial evidence to make it admissible, a witness need only give an indication as to when, where, and under what circumstances the photograph was taken, and that the photograph accurately portrays the subject illustrated. General questions as to the admission or rejection of pictorial evidence, and also of the sufficiency of identification of pictorial evidence, lie within the sound discretion of the trial court. Questions raised which attack the accuracy of the pictorial evidence sought to be introduced go to the weight of the evidence, and not to its admissibility. In this case, Pentecost's testimony gave some indication that the picture in question accurately portrayed the person cashing the check, and testified as to the circumstances under which the photograph was taken. Coupled with Dale's testimony as to the Regiscope process, there was sufficient authentication to warrant admitting the Regiscope photograph into evidence. Affirmed.

EDITOR'S ANALYSIS: The theory behind the admission of photographic evidence is that photographs are merely graphic representations of oral testimony, hence the need for verification. Some courts have taken this theory further, holding that photographic evidence is illustrative, not substantive, resulting in the exclusion of photographic evidence from the jury room. This distinction is generally held to be groundless, and does not handle recent developments in photographic technology very well.

PEOPLE v. BOWLEY

Sp. Ct. of Cal., 1963. 59 Cal. 2d 855, 31 Cal Rptr. 471, 382 P. 2d 591, Noted, 62 Mich. L. Rev. 1259

NATURE OF CASE: Appeal from conviction of oral copulation.

FACT SUMMARY: The testimony of Bowley's (D) accomplice laid the foundation for the introduction into evidence of a film purporting to show Bowley (D) and the accomplice engaging in oral copulation. The film was the only evidence corroborative of the accomplice's testimony.

CONCISE RULE OF LAW: A photograph may, in a proper case, be admitted into evidence, not merely as illustrative testimony of a human witness, but as probative evidence in itself of what it shows.

FACTS: Bowley's (D) accomplice was the only witness against him. Her (the accomplice's) testimony laid the foundation for the introduction into evidence of a film purporting to show her and Bowley (D) engaging in oral copulation. The film was the only evidence offered to corroborate the accomplice's testimony, and her testimony was the only foundation offered for its admission.

ISSUE: Can a film be used to corroborate an accomplice's testimony where the film's admission into evidence rested solely upon the accomplice's foundation testimony?

HOLDING AND DECISION: No. First of all the fact that the foundation for the introduction of a film into evidence was laid by an accomplice is not a ground for objecting to its admittance. Secondly a photograph may, in a proper case, be admitted into evidence not merely as illustrated testimony of a human witness but as probative evidence in itself of what it shows. But because the film here was properly admitted into evidence, and because that film is properly authenticated is of itself evidence of what it depicts. It does not follow that the film can corroborate the testimony of the sole authenticating witness when she is an accomplice. A film becomes probative only after if has been authenticated. Here that authentication came from the accomplice whose testimony the film was to corroborate. The authentication of a film offered to corroborate an accomplice's testimony must come from a source independent of the accomplice. Bowley's (D) conviction is reversed.

EDITOR'S ANALYSIS: According to Wigmore a photograph is no more than the non-verbal expression of the witness upon whose foundation testimony its authenticity rests. It is merely that witness's testimony in illustrated form. Other authorities, such as the Bowley court disagree. They urge that photographs may be used as probative evidence of what they depict. Used in this manner they take on the status of independent "silent" witnesses. However, as Bowley indicates, whichever way photographs are used, they must be authenticated.

NOTES:

COMMONWEALTH v. REAGEN

175 Mass. 335, 56 N.E. 577 (1900)

NATURE OF CASE: Not included in casebook excerpt.

FACT SUMMARY: Reagen (D) was convicted and appealed, claiming that questions as to a witness's competency to testify were improperly left to the jury.

CONCISE RULE OF LAW: It is the duty of the trial judge in a jury trial to resolve all questions as to a witness's competency to testify, and to reject witnesses he finds incompetent to testify.

FACTS: At Reagen's (D) trial, upon voir dire examination, the judge was of the opinion that a witness was incompetent to testify. He made no formal order or ruling on competency. The witness was sworn and allowed to testify over Reagen's (D) objections that the witness did not understand the nature of the oath, the judge stating he should leave the question of the witness's competency to the jury. The judge instructed the jury that if they found the witness competent they should consider her testimony as evidence, if not, to disregard her testimony. The jury found the witness competent and relied in part on her testimony. Reagen (D) was convicted and appealed.

ISSUE: Is it the duty of the trial judge in a jury trial to resolve all questions as to a witness's competency to testify and to reject witnesses he finds incompetent to testify?

HOLDING AND DECISION: (Hammond, J.) Yes. It is the duty of the trial judge in a jury trial to resolve all questions as to a witness's competency to testify and to reject witnesses he finds incompetent to testify. Generally, in a jury trial, all questions as to the admissibility of evidence are for the judge. Especially in criminal cases where the objection to a witness's competency is based upon the witness's ability to understand the nature of the oath, the danger is great that if the question of competency is left to the jury, the decision will be made in part on the nature of the testimony offered by the challenged witness. Leaving such questions to the judge contributes to the orderly and efficient conduct of a trial. If the witness's competency is challenged on the grounds that because of youthfulness or insanity he does not understand the nature of the oath, the judge should examine the witness's competency, and reject the witness unless the court finds him competent to testify. In this case, the judge was of the opinion that the witness was not competent. She should have been rejected as a witness; it was error to submit the question of competency to the jury. The jury relied on the testimony, and assuming that the testimony was prejudicial to Reagen (D), it cannot be said error was harmless. Verdict set aside.

EDITOR'S ANALYSIS: The rule today is quite different in federal courts. In federal courts, there is no competency exception for small children or insane persons, the court rather lets in the evidence for what its worth, with proper cautionary instructions. Objections would go to the witness's credibility, and these matters need not be raised before the witness testifies.

NOTES:

JACKSON v. DENNO

378 U.S. 368 (1964)

NATURE OF CASE: Writ of habeus corpus challenging the validity of a murder conviction.

FACT SUMMARY: Jackson (D) filed a writ of habeus corpus in federal court, asserting that his conviction for murder was invalid because it was founded upon a confession not properly determined to be voluntary.

CONCISE RULE OF LAW: A defendant in a criminal trial who challenges the voluntariness of a confession offered into evidence against him is entitled to a fair hearing in which the voluntariness of his confession is accurately and reliably determined.

FACTS: At approximately 1:00 A.M. on June 14, 1960, Jackson (D) robbed a hotel clerk. When he left the hotel, he encountered a policeman. A struggle ensued in which the policeman was killed, and Jackson (D) was shot twice. Jackson (D) got a cab which took him to the hospital. While there, at approximately 2:00 A.M., Jackson (D) confessed to the murder and the shooting in response to a detective's questioning. At 3:55 A.M., after being administered drugs and after having lost 500 c.c. of blood, Jackson (D) was interrogated by an assistant district attorney, in the presence of police officers and hospital personnel. Despite protesting that he could not go on, upon further questioning, Jackson (D) admitted to shooting the policeman and having fired the first shot. Jackson (D) was indicted, and at trial, the statements made by him at the hospital were admitted without objection. Jackson (D) took the stand on his own behalf, and his account differed in some important aspects from the confession. Testimony was heard on both sides on the issue of whether Jackson (D) had been pressured into answering questions. According to state practice, the voluntariness issue was submitted to the jury, along with the other issues of the case. The jury was instructed to disregard the confession entirely if it found it involuntary, and if it found that it was voluntary, to determine its truth or reliability and afford it weight accordingly. Jackson (D) was convicted of first degree murder, and Jackson (D) filed a writ of habeus corpus challenging the constitutionality of the state practice. The writ was denied by the district court, and the Court of Appeals affirmed Jackson's (D) conviction. Certiorari was then granted to review the constitutionality of the state practice involved.

ISSUE: Is a defendant in a criminal trial who challenges the voluntariness of a confession offered into evidence against him entitled to a fair hearing in which the voluntariness of the confession is accurately and reliably determined?

HOLDING AND DECISION: (White, J.) Yes. A defendant in a criminal trial who challenges the voluntariness of a confession offered into evidence against him is entitled to a fair hearing in which the voluntariness of the confession is accurately and reliably determined. A criminal defendant is deprived of due process of law if his conviction is based in any part upon an involuntary confession, regardless of truth or falsity of the confession or the sufficiency of other evidence against him. Precedent is clear that the defendant has the constitutional right to challenge the use of a confession, and to have the voluntariness issue resolved, uninfluenced by the truth or falsity of the confession. The state practice involved here does not provide for this reliable determination and is therefore constitutionally infirm. Under the state practice, if an issue of coercion is presented, the judge may not make the determination of voluntariness, but must leave it for the jury to decide. The issue is submitted to the jury along with all the other issues of the case, there is no definite, open, and separate determination of the voluntariness issue. To allow the issue to be determined in light of all the other evidence injects irrelevant and impermissible considerations of truthfulness into the assessment of voluntariness. Even if under the state practice the jury found that the confession was involuntary, it would be impossible to show that the confession was not relied on. At the very least, Jackson (D) is entitled to a full evidentiary hearing where a reliable solution is made on the voluntariness issue. Reversed and remanded.

DISSENT: (Black, J.) The court, in stating that only a reliable determination on the voluntariness issue will satisfy constitutional requirements, implicitly infers that jury's findings on this question are inherently unreliable. The decision effectively removes this issue from the province of the jury, requiring the judge to make this determination. Given the Court's lack of guidance on the issue of the burden of proof required of judges to find voluntariness, such a decision could present distinct disadvantages to the criminal defendant.

EDITOR'S ANALYSIS: A reading of Jackson finding a requirement that the determination of voluntariness must be made outside of the jury's presence is an oversimplification. So long as the hearing is adequate, fairly held, and does not cause the jury to hear testimony it was not entitled to hear, a hearing in the jury's presence on the voluntariness issue does not violate due process. See Pinto v. Pierce 389 U.S. 31 (1967).

NOTES:

LEGO v. TWOMEY

SUPR.CT.OF U.S., 1972. 404 U.S.553, 92 S.Ct.619, 30 L.Ed.2d 618

NATURE OF CASE: **Appeal from conviction for robbery.**

FACT SUMMARY: **Lego (P) was convicted of robbery based on a confession he made to police after arrest. Lego (P) claims the confession was not voluntary, but beaten out of him.**

CONCISE RULE OF LAW: **When a confession challenged as involuntary is sought to be used against a criminal defendant at his trial, he is entitled to a reliable and clear-cut determination that the confession was, in fact, voluntarily rendered as shown by a preponderance of the evidence.**

FACTS: Lego (P) was convicted of armed robbery. The evidence introduced at trial included a confession made by him to police after his arrest and while in their custody. Lego claimed that the confession was involuntary. The trial judge conducted a hearing, out of the presence of the jury, to determine whether the confession was voluntary. He ruled it voluntary and thus admissible. Lego (P) appealed his conviction to the Illinois Supreme Court but lost. Four years later, Lego (P) challenged his conviction by seeking a writ of habeas corpus in the United States District Court. He contended that the trial judge should have found the confession voluntary "beyond a reasonable doubt" before admitting it. Illinois law provided that the judge should determine the voluntariness question by a preponderance of the evidence. Lego (P) also argued that the voluntariness issue should have been submitted to the jury for its separate consideration. The District Court denied relief on the merits and the Court of Appeals for the Seventh Circuit affirmed.

ISSUE: Does the judge have to find a confession voluntary beyond a reasonable doubt before allowing it in evidence?

HOLDING AND DECISION: No. A defendant in a criminal case is deprived of due process of law if his conviction is founded, in whole or in part, upon an involuntary confession, regardless of whether the confession was true or false. The voluntariness hearing was established to safeguard the right of an individual not to be compelled to condemn himself by his own utterances. The hearing has nothing whatever to do with improving the reliability of jury verdicts. The accused cannot be convicted except upon proof beyond a reasonable doubt of every fact necessary to constitute the crime he is charged with. A confession is not an element of the crime and thus this standard does not apply to confessions. A less stringent standard may be adopted, as here, where only a preponderance of the evidence is necessary. The accused is entitled to a reliable and clear-cut determination that the confession was, in fact, voluntarily made. This was done by the judge in the case at bar. The prosecution must prove the voluntariness by a preponderance of the evidence only. Each state is free to adopt a higher standard. There is also no merit in Lego's (P) assertion that the jury should be allowed to separately decide the voluntariness issue. The Court of Appeals is affirmed.

DISSENT: (Brennan, J.) Previous cases have reflected the concern over the use of involuntary confessions in criminal trials. The use of a preponderance standard at an evidentiary hearing on the voluntariness issue does not provide sufficient protection against that danger and is tantamount to saying that it is no more serious in general to admit involuntary confessions in criminal trials than it is to exclude voluntary ones.

EDITOR'S ANALYSIS: The sole issue to be determined in a voluntariness hearing is whether or not a confession was coerced. The truth or falsity of the confession is irrelevant at this hearing, and it is, in fact, improper to inqurie into this issue. The judge is not permitted to take into consideration evidence which would indicate that the confession, though involuntary, is reliable. This may often be a difficult task.

NOTES:

SILVER v. NEW YORK CENTRAL RAILROAD CO.

SUP. JUD. COURT OF MASSACHUSETTS, 1952.
329 Mass. 14, 105 N.E. 2d 923

NOTES:

NATURE OF CASE: Action for damages for personal injuries resulting from low temperature.

FACT SUMMARY: In order to prove that the temperature on New York Central's (D) train was not too low, New York Central (D) sought to introduce evidence that no one else complained to the porter of the lack of heat.

CONCISE RULE OF LAW: Evidence of no complaints is too remote to show a lack of defect unless there is evidence of similar circumstances of the persons not complaining, and that they had an opportunity to complain.

FACTS: Silver (P) has alleged that an ailment she has was worsened because the temperature on New York Central's (D) railroad car was too low. In order to prove that the temperature was not too low, New York Central (D) sought to have the porter testify that none of the other passengers complained of the cold. The court would not allow this evidence.

ISSUE: Does the hearsay rule prevent evidence of the lack of complaints to show the lack of a defect?

HOLDING AND DECISION: No. The hearsay rule does not prevent such testimony. However, such evidence should be considered to be too remote, and inadmissible, unless the non-complaining parties were in a similar position as the plaintiff, and they had an adequate opportunity to complain. In this case, the passengers on the train were all in a similar position with Silver (P), and it is not likely that they would refrain from complaining if the temperature dropped below what was proper. The porter was also the proper person to testify to such matters because he would be the person that would probably hear the complaints. Therefore, as there was an opportunity for the passengers to complain, the evidence of the lack of complaints was wrongfully excluded from evidence.

EDITOR'S ANALYSIS: The situation in this case, and the food situation the court talked about are the classic areas in which a silence is the basis of an affirmative inference. While some courts have treated such cases as hearsay, most courts ignore any hearsay problem and base exclusion solely on relevancy. This is the way this court handled the problem. This explains the large number of courts which allow the lack of complaints to be admitted to show the lack of a defective condition. The trend is in the direction of admitting such evidence as non-hearsay. This trend finds support in recent statutes and rules.

UNITED STATES v. DAY

591 F.2d 861 (D.C. Cir. 1978)

NATURE OF CASE: Appeal from ruling excluding evidence as hearsay.

FACT SUMMARY: The testimony of the government's (P) witness that the victim had given a witness a slip of paper with Day's (D) name and phone number with instructions to give it to the police should he fail to return (prior to his being murdered) was held to be inadmissible hearsay.

CONCISE RULE OF LAW: Testimony describing another's actions observed directly by the witness does not constitute hearsay and is admissible.

FACTS: The murder victim, Williams, gave the witness, Mason, a slip of paper with Day's (D) name and phone number. After telling Mason about a fight between Day (D) and himself over possession of some guns and that Williams feared Day (D) because Day (D) was out to get him, Williams instructed Mason to give the police the information on the slip of paper if he did not return by 3:00 p.m. the next day. When Williams failed to return, Mason phoned the police who later found Williams' body. Mason's testimony of these facts for the government (P) at Day's (D) murder trial was excluded as hearsay. The government (P) appealed.

ISSUE: Does testimony of another person's actions directly observed by the witness constitute hearsay?

HOLDING AND DECISION: (C.J. MacKinnon) No. Mason's testimony describing Williams' act of giving him a slip of paper with Day's (D) name and phone number on it is admissible because it was observed directly by Mason, the witness, and thus it is not hearsay. Because the information on the paper was offered only to show that Wiliams was associated with Day (D), which is an inference drawn from Williams' act in giving the paper to Mason, it is also not hearsay. If, however, the information on the paper were offered to prove that the phone number written on the paper was, in fact, Day's (D) phone number, the paper's contents would be hearsay. Mason's testimony of what Williams stated to be Day's (D) motives for wanting to harm Williams is inadmissible hearsay. But because it was used to prove that Williams feared Day (D), it is admissible as a state of mind exception to the hearsay rule.

DISSENT: (J. Robinson) Association between Day (D) and Williams can only be shown if Williams did in fact write Day's (D) real number on the slip of paper. If the writing on the paper is not offered for the truth of whether Williams knew Day (D) well enough to know Day's (D) phone number, it is not hearsay, but still inadmissible because it is irrelevant. If the writing is offered for its truth, it is hearsay and inadmissible. The majority holds that merely the act of giving Mason the paper with Day's (D) name on it and some phone number is sufficient to show association. In reality, the probative value of proving association is quite small compared to its prejudicial effect against Day (D). The government (P) already had much stronger evidence to prove association. Because the probative value of this evidence is outweighed by the prejudicial effect of a jury inferring that Williams expected Day (D) to do him great harm just before Williams was murdered (instead of merely inferring that Williams knew Day (D)), he court should exercise its discretion under Federal Rules of Evidence 403 and not allow otherwise admissible evidence merely because of its prejudicial effect.

EDITOR'S ANALYSIS: In determining whether evidence is hearsay and, if it is hearsay, whether it is admissible under an hearsay exception, it is important to note what the evidence is offered to prove. The purpose claimed can at times be so limited (in order to avoid having the evidence categorized as hearsay) that the evidentiary purpose is either irrelevant or has too little probative value to justify its prejudicial effect.

NOTES:

JENKINS v. ANDERSON, WARDEN

Sup. Ct. of U.S., 447 U.S. 231. 100 Sup. Ct. 2124 (1980)

NATURE OF CASE: Appeal from a manslaughter conviction.

FACT SUMMARY: Jenkins (D) contended the prosecution violated his Fifth Amendment right to remain silent when it impeached his self defense argument by informing the jury that after killing the victim, he did not surrender to the police for two weeks.

CONCISE RULE OF LAW: The use of pre-arrest silence to impeach a defendant's credibility does not violate the Fifth or Fourteenth Amendments.

FACTS: Jenkins (D) was charged with manslaughter after he stabbed Redding. At trial he testified that he stabbed Redding in self-defense. On cross examination, the prosecution questioned him as to why he remained silent and failed to report the incident to police for two weeks. The prosecution brought Jenkin's (D) silence up again in its closing argument. Jenkins (D) was convicted and appealed, contending the use of his silence to impeach him, violated his Fifth Amendment right to remain silent and his Fourteenth Amendment right to fundamental fairness.

ISSUE: Does the use of pre-arrest silence to impeach a defendant's credibility violate either the Fifth or Fourteenth Amendments?

HOLDING AND DECISION: (J. Powell) No. The use of pre-arrest silence to impeach a defendant's credibility does not violate either the Fifth or the Fourteenth Amendments. A defendant who chooses to testify in his own defense waives his right to silence and subjects himself to cross examination on subjects reasonably related to his testimony. The Fifth Amendment right covers the right not to give information about yourself. It does not apply to pre-arrest silence. Further, the Fourteenth Amendment does not aborgate the common law rule that witnessess may be impeached by their previous failure to state a fact in circumstances in which that fact naturally would have been revealed. In this case it is reasonable to assert that one who kills in self-defense would assert that defense to the police at his first opportunity. As a result, Jenkins (D) was not denied any constitutional rights. Affirmed.

DISSENT: (Marshall, J.) The court's broad holding today that a criminal defendant's testimony may be impeached by pre-arrest silence has three fatal defects. First, the probative value of pre-arrest silence is so small that to allow it's use for impeachment purposes violates due process. Second, the availability of drawing upon an adverse inference from pre-arrest silence infringes the privilege against self-incrimination. Finally, the availability of such an adverse inference for impeachment purposes impermissibly burdens the defendant's decision to testify on his/her own behalf.

EDITOR'S ANALYSIS: This case, illustrates the scope of the prosecution's ability to impeach a defendant with his own action or inaction. The Fifth Amendment protections have been asserted against the use of testimony obtained in violation of it. However, such testimony may be used in impeaching the witness. Impeachment is considered of paramount importance as it relates to the credibility of evidence, and the ability to impeach is not often restricted.

NOTES:

MAHLANDT v. WILD CANID SURVIVAL & REEARCH CENTER, INC.
U.S. Ct. of Apls., 8th Cir., 1978, 588 F.2d 626

NATURE OF CASE: Appeal from denial of damages for negligence.

FACT SUMMARY: The trial court hearing Daniel Mahlandt's (P) civil action against the Center (D) refused to let into evidence certain conclusionary statements against interest made by an employee of the Center (D).

CONCISE RULE OF LAW: Federal Rule of Evidence 801(d)(2)(D) makes statements made by agents within the scope of their employment admissible and there is no implied requirement that the declarant have personal knowledge of the facts underlying his statement.

FACTS: Nobody actually saw what happened, but young Daniel Mahlandt (P), who was just under four-years-old at the time, wound up in the enclosure where Mr. Poos (D), the Director of the Center (D), kept Sophie—a wolf belonging to the Center (D) but which he took around to schools and institutions where he showed films and gave programs regarding the nature of wolves. Sophie had been raised at the children's zoo and had there acted in a good natured and stable manner while in contact with thousands of children. Sophie apparently bit Mahlandt (P) causing him serious injuries. There was some evidence indicating that the child might have crawled under the fence and thereby received his injuries. An offer was made to disprove this theory by introducing evidence that Poos (D) had left a note on the door of the Center's (D) president saying the wolf had bitten a child and that he had made a similar statement later that day when he met the president and was asked what happened. There was also an offer to introduce minutes of a meeting of the Center's (D) board that reflected a great deal of discussion about the legal aspects of the incident of Sophie biting the child. None of this was let into evidence, the judge reasoning that in each case those making the statements had no personal knowledge of the facts and the statements were thus hearsay. A judgment for the Center (D) followed.

ISSUE: Is it necessary to show that the agent had personal knowledge of the facts underlining his statement for a statement made by an agent within the scope of his employment to be admissible under Federal Rule of Evidence 801(d)(2)(D)?

HOLDING AND DECISION: (J. Van Sickle) No. Federal Rule of Evidence 801(d)(2)(D) makes admissible statements made by agents within the scope of their employment. Rule 403 provides for the exclusion of relevant evidence if its probative value is substantially outweighed by the danger of unfair prejudice, etc. Rule 805 recites, in effect, that a statement containing hearsay within hearsay is admissible if each part of the statement falls within an exception to the hearsay rule. While each provides additional bases for excluding otherwise acceptable evidence, neither rule mandates the introduction into Rule 801(d)(2)(D) of an implied requirement that the declarant have personal knowledge of the facts underlying his statement. Thus, the two statements made by Poos (D) (one in the note he wrote and one he made verbally) were admissible against the Center (D). As to the minutes of the Center's (D) board meeting, there was no servant or agency relationship which justified admitting the evidence of these minutes as against Poos (D) (who was a non-attending, non-participating employee). The only remaining question is whether the trial court's rulings excluding these three items of evidence are at all justified under Rule 403. It is true that none of the statements involved were based on the personal knowledge of the declarant. However, it was recognized by the Advisory Committee on Proposed Rules that this does not necessarily mean they must be rejected as too unreliable to be admitted into evidence. In its discussion of 801(d)(2) exceptions to the hearsay rule, the Committee said: "The freedom which admissions have enjoyed from technical demands of searching for an assurance of trustworthiness in some against-interest circumstances, and form the restrictive influences of the opinion rule and the rule requiring first-hand knowledge, when taken with the apparently prevalent satisfaction with the results, calls for generous treatment of this avenue to admissibility." 28 U.S.C.A., Volume of Federal Rules of Evidence, Rule 801, p. 527, at p. 530. So here, remembering that relevant evidence is usually prejudicial to the cause of the side against which it is presented, and that the prejudice which concerns us is unreasonable prejudice—and applying the spirit of Rule 801(d)(2)—Rule 403 does not warrant the exclusion of the evidence of Poos' (D) statements as against himself or the Center (D). But the limited admissibility of the corporate minutes, coupled with the repetitive nature of the evidence and the low probative value of the minute record, all justify supporting the judgment of the trial court, under Rule 403, not to admit them into evidence. Reversed and remanded for a new trial.

EDITOR'S ANALYSIS: One of the questions courts have struggled with in this area is whether or not in order to quality as an admission the statement must have been made by the agent to an outsider (i.e., one other than his principal or another agent). This often comes up when the opposing party in a suit against the principal wants to introduce into evidence a report written or given orally by an agent to the principal or another agent. Just as many courts have refused to let such evidence in as have let it in against the principal as an admission. The Federal Rules of Evidence have been interpreted as recognizing what Wigmore observed: that "communication to an outsider has not generally been thought to be an essential characteristic of an admission." v Wigmore on Evidence, section 1557.

NOTES:

UNITED STATES v. FLOYD

555 F.2d 45 (2nd Cir. 1977), cert. den., 434 U.S. 851

NATURE OF CASE: Appeal from conviction for armed robbery.

FACT SUMMARY: Floyd (D) was convicted on the hearsay testimony of a witness who, after the actual conspiratorial act of robbing a bank had been completed, had heard Floyd's (D) co-conspirator admit that Floyd (D) and he had robbed a bank.

CONCISE RULE OF LAW: The conspiracy to commit a crime must still be in operation to admit a co-conspirator's statement into evidence against a defendant under the co-conspirator hearsay exception.

FACTS: Floyd (D) escaped identification by guards and bank cameras by wearing a Halloween mask while robbing a bank. Floyd (D) and his girlfriend presented an alibi to counter incriminating testimony by the getaway car driver who was the government's (P) chief witness. However, Floyd's (D) co-conspirator had admitted to Duffy, while destroying the getaway car the day after the robbery, that Floyd (D) and he had robbed a bank. Duffy testified to the co-conspirator's out-of-court statement, and Floyd (D) was convicted. Floyd (D) appealed the trial court's decision to admit Duffy's hearsay testimony against Floyd (D).

ISSUE: Must the conspiracy still be in existence to admit a co-conspirator's out-of-court admission against a defendant under the co-conspirator exception to the hearsay rule?

HOLDING AND DECISION: (J. Coffrin) Yes. The established rule is that once the main purpose of the conspiracy is attained, a subsidiary conspiracy to conceal the crime may not be implied to later acts. Here as in Grunewald v. United States, to rule otherwise would eliminate any sense of when a conspiracy ends. The destruction of the getaway car was outside the bounds of the conspiracy to rob a bank. Therefore, Floyd's (D) co-conspirator's admission was not admissible under the co-conspirator hearsay exception, Federal Rules of Evidence, Rule 801(d)(2)(E).

EDITOR'S ANALYSIS: The issue of how broad is the definition of conspiracy in Rule 801(d)(2)(E) actually has two components. First, any statement made by a conspirator while engaged in an act during and in furtherance of the central purpose of the crime being charged is admissible against any conspirator. Second, under Federal Rules of Evidence, Rule 104(a), the court, rather than a jury under Rule 104(b), decides whether any actions taken after the central criminal purpose had been achieved are part of the conspiracy.

NOTES:

UNITED STATES v. VINSON
606 F.2d 149 (6th Cir. 1979)

NATURE OF CASE: Appeal from conviction for extortion.

FACT SUMMARY: **The trial court allowed hearsay testimony containing a co-conspirator's admission of extortion to be presented against both conspirators, Vinson (D) and Thompson (D), in front of the jury before the government (P) had proven the existence of a conspiracy later.**

CONCISE RULE OF LAW: **(1) It is permissible for a trial court to allow hearsay testimony in front of a jury prior to hearing the foundational evidence for the hearsay exception, and ruling on the admissibility of the hearsay testimony later after the foundational evidence is presented. (2) The trial court may consider the hearsay testimony presented earlier in the trial when deciding later if sufficient foundational evidence has been offered to admit the hearsay testimony.**

FACTS: An officer of coal company testified of Sheriff Vinson's (D) admission that he and his co-conspirator, Magistrate Thompson (D), were working together in an extortion scheme against the coal company. Using the co-conspirator statement exception to the hearsay rule, the trial judge allowed the company officer's testimony to be presented to the jury before the government (P) had proven the necessary foundation that a conspiracy had existed when Vinson's (D) admission was made. After the government (P) had proven the existence of a conspiracy between Vinson (D) and Thompson (D), the trial judge found that a conspiracy was proven and formally admitted the testimony of the company officer. Vinson (D) appealed.

ISSUES: (1) May hearsay evidence be presented to a jury prior to the presentation of foundational evidence and prior to a ruling on the admissibility of the hearsay evidence? (2) May the trial court consider hearsay testimony presented in court but not yet admitted into the record when deciding later on in the trial whether the foundational evidence offered to admit the same hearsay testimony is sufficient?

HOLDING AND DECISION: (J. Merrit) (1) Yes. In its discretion, the court may allow the company officer to testify about Vinson's (D) admission against both Vinson (D) and Thompson (D), even though Thompson (D) was not yet shown to be linked to Vinson (D) in a conspiracy, as long as the court could anticipate the presentation, later on in the trial, of foundational evidence showing a conspiracy and be able to rule on the admissibility of the testimony at that time. (2) Yes. A judge may consider evidence such as hearsay even if it has not been admitted when deciding whether to admit evidence. When a judge decides questions of admissibility of evidence based on whether sufficient foundation has been shown for the evidence (under Federal Rules of Evidence, Rule 104(a)), the judge is not bound by the rules of evidence.

EDITOR'S ANALYSIS: The trial judge must weigh each party's need for flexibility in order to make an effective presentation of his case, with the need to protect the defendant from being prejudiced by injecting inadmissible evidence into the record. (Once something incriminating is said before a jury, a judge's instruction to ignore it will not necessarily prevent the jury from at least subconsciously considering what was said.) This case also recognized the large amount of discretion allowed a judge in deciding whether evidence should be admitted.

NOTES:

RUHALA v. ROBY

SUP. COURT OF MICHIGAN, 1967.
379 Mich. 102, 150 N.W. 2d 146

NATURE OF CASE: Civil action for damages for wrongful death.

FACT SUMMARY: After Esther Kingsley was killed in a collision with Burditt's (D) truck, Burditt first claimed Roby (D) was driving Esther's car; but at trial he claimed Esther was "behind the wheel" at the time of the accident.

CONCISE RULE OF LAW: Evidence of a prior inconsistent statement for purposes of impeachment is not substantive evidence unless the witness admits at trial that the prior inconsistent statement is true.

FACTS: Esther Kingsley was killed when her car collided with Burditt's (D) truck. Roby (D) was in the car with Esther. Ruhala (P), administrator of Esther Kingsley's estate, alleged that Roby (D) was driving Esther's car at the time of the accident. Roby (D) denied this, claiming Esther's negligent driving was the cause of the accident. Shortly after the accident, Burditt (D) had told a policeman that a man had been driving Esther's car when the collision occurred. He once later affirmed this. But in an even later deposition, and at trial, Burditt (D) stated that immediately prior to the collision, it was his "impression" that "a woman was behind the wheel." At trial, the court precluded Ruhala (P) from proving Burditt's (D) inconsistent statements. Ruhala (P) appealed.

ISSUE: Is a prior inconsistent statement substantive evidence where it is offered for purposes of impeaching a witness?

HOLDING AND DECISION: No. There are only two instances where a prior inconsistent statement may be used as substantive evidence: (1) where the witness adopts the prior inconsistent statement as true at trial, and (2) as an admission of a party opponent that qualifies as an exception to the hearsay rule. Burditt (D) did not adopt his prior inconsistent statements as true. Since admissions of one defendant (Burditt) are not admissible into evidence against a co-defendant (Roby), Burditt's (D) prior inconsistent statements, even if admissions, are not admissible against Roby (D). Thus, the court here precluded Ruhala (P) from using Burditt's (D) prior inconsistent statements as substantive evidence to prove whether or not Roby (D) was driving Esther Kingsley's car at the time of the accident. However, the court also refused such evidence for impeachment purposes against Burditt (D).

EDITOR'S ANALYSIS: Several writers have criticized the general rule in this case. Judge Learned Hand felt that juries would have no trouble weighing the probative value of a prior inconsistent statement against a statement at trial under oath. And McCormick sees prior inconsistent statements as possibly more reliable than the statement at trial, since they were made on fresher memory due to their closeness to the fact. Both views raise the argument that prior inconsistent statements should be given substantive effect; i.e., as tending to prove the truth of what was said. They contend that since the declarant is on the stand, subject to cross-examination under oath, this precludes any hearsay problems with prior extra-judicial statements.

The underlying problem that this case points up is the difficulty courts have with jury interpretation of prior inconsistent statements admitte d as evidence. Juries tend to treat all evidence as substantive. However, the majority of courts feel that the prejudicial effect prior inconsistent statements can have on jury verdicts should in some way be limited. Thus, evidence of such statements only goes to the credibility of the declaring witness, not toward proving the major issues of the case.

NOTES:

WHITEHURST v. WRIGHT

592 F.2d 834 (5th Cir. 1979)

NATURE OF CASE: Civil right action under 42 U.S.C. 1983.

FACT SUMMARY: In a civil rights action, arising from an incident in which police shot an innocent man whom they mistook to be a robber, Whitehurst (P) was not allowed to impeach her own witness in order to refute Wright's (D) claim that the victim shot first.

CONCISE RULE OF LAW: Impeachment of testimony by prior inconsistent statement may not be permitted where employed as mere subterfuge to get before the jury evidence not otherwise admissible.

FACTS: The decedent was gunned down by a policeman who mistook him for a robber. The policeman claimed that the decedent shot first, but none of the officers in the area found a gun near the body. A detective arriving later found a gun confiscated by police in a drug raid one year earlier laying 27 inches from the body. Whitehurst (P), decedent's survivor, tried to show that the detective planted the gun there to defeat any lawsuit against the police. Whitehurst (P) called the detective as her witness and allowed him to testify that he found the gun there with one spent round. Whitehurst (P) then sought to impeach the detective's testimony with the testimony of another officer who claimed the detective told him that he had fired the gun once. Whitehurst (P) argued that the trial court erroneously prevented her from impeaching her witness.

ISSUE: May testimony be impeached merely to get otherwise inadmissible evidence before a jury?

HOLDING AND DECISION: (J. Vance) No. Testimony may not be impeached solely to get otherwise inadmissible evidence before a jury. Whitehurst (P) purposely called an adverse witness whose testimony could only hurt her case. While the Federal Rules of Evidence do allow a party to impeach his own witness under Rule 607 and while prior inconsistent statements are allowable to impeach, it is an abuse of the prior inconsistent statements hearsay exception to call a witness solely to impeach him.

EDITOR'S ANALYSIS: The use of prior inconsistent statements serves only to negate prior testimony and thereby keep a witness honest in a trial. These statements cannot be offered to prove the truth of the prior inconsistencies which they contain.

NOTES:

SHEPARD v. UNITED STATES

290 U.S. 96 (1933)

NATURE OF CASE: Appeal from conviction for murder.

FACT SUMMARY: Shepard (D) filed a writ of certiori challenging the validity of his murder conviction, claiming that the court improperly admitted evidence of a dying declaration of his prejudice.

CONCISE RULE OF LAW: In order for a statement to be considered a dying declaration, the declarant must have spoken without hope of recovery and in the shadow of impending death.

FACTS: Shepard (D) was convicted of murdering his wife by poisoning. Two days after Mrs. Shepard had become ill, while she was lying in bed, she had a conversation with Brown, a nurse. Mrs. Shepard asked Brown to bring her a particular bottle of liquor, told Brown that that was what she was drinking right before she collapsed, asked Brown to test it for poison, and then stated, "Dr. Shepard (D) has poisoned me." The conversation was admitted after Brown testified that Mrs. Shepard said she was not going to get well, that she was going to die. At the time the conversation took place, all prospects for Mrs. Shepard's recovery were good. A fortnight after the conversation, Mrs. Shepard gave an indication that she was still hopeful of recovery. Shepard (D) was convicted, and the conviction was affirmed by the Court of Appeals. Shepard (D) then filed a writ of certiorari.

ISSUE: In order for a statement to be considered a dying declaration, must the declarant have spoken without hope of recovery and in the shadow of impending death?

HOLDING AND DECISION: (Cardozo, J.) Yes. In order for a statement to be considered a dying declaration, the declarant must have spoken without hope of recovery and in the shadow of impending death. Fear or even belief that illness will result in death will not suffice. There must be a "settled" hopeless expectation that death Is near at hand, and what Is said must have been spoken in hush of its impending presence. Here, there was hope for recovery, and death was not imminent when the statement was made, and therefore it could not have been admitted as a dying declaration. It cannot be said that the admission of the declaration was mere unsubstantial error.

EDITOR'S ANALYSIS: There is no reason to believe that fear or even belief that one is going to die could not provide the guarantee of special reliability necessary to admit this type of hearsay evidence, since it is probably reasonable that persons so inclined would tell the truth. The strict application of the doctrine probably represents a basic lack of trust in "deathbed" statements generally.

NOTES:

GOLDSTEIN v. SKLAR

216 A.2d 298 (1966)

NATURE OF CASE: Appeal from award of damages for personal injuries.

FACT SUMMARY: Although Goldstein (P) himself could not testify, Goldstein's (P) doctor was allowed to support his diagnosis of Goldstein's (P) injuries by testifying that Goldstein (P) had told him of being thrown to the left in the auto collision even though his testimony might influence the jury in deciding the fault of the accident.

CONCISE RULE OF LAW: A doctor treating a patient can testify to the patient's medical history as related to him by the patient only to support his diagnosis of the condition sustained by the victim after the injury, but not to establish the fault of the injury.

FACTS: Goldstein (P) and Sklar (D) were allegedly involved in an accident causing injury to Goldstein (P). Goldstein (P) was unable to testify. Instead, Goldstein's (P) doctor testified about Goldstein's description of Goldstein's (P) injuries in order to prove his diagnosis of the type of injury Goldstein (P) sustained, including the fact that Goldstein (P) had told the doctor that he had been thrown to the left in the collision. Sklar (D) claimed that his description served to establish fault and was not necessary for a diagnosis. Sklar (D) appealed judgment for Goldstein (P).

ISSUE: May a doctor's testimony include hearsay evidence of his patient's impressions and conditions as described by his patient, to support the doctor's diagnosis of his patient's injury?

HOLDING AND DECISION: (J. Dufresne) Yes. A doctor may testify about statements made to the doctor by a person describing his own condition and sensations to substantiate the doctor's diagnosis. Presumably, a person desiring successful medical care would be truthful to his doctor. The doctor's testimony relating to Goldstein's (P) description of being thrown to the left is admissible to support the doctor's diagnosis of injuries to the left side of Goldstein's (P) body. However, because the doctor's testimony of Goldstein's (P) account of the accident can only be used as a medical history to support a diagnosis, the trial judge must instruct the jury not to consider the doctor's testimony of Goldstein's being thrown to the left as evidence that Sklar (D) struck Goldstein's (P) car from the left and was thus negligent. The trial judge made this cautionary instruction.

EDITOR'S ANALYSIS: Only because of the strong likelihood of truthfulness, courts will admit a doctor's hearsay testimony of his patient's description of an accident made in the course of a professional medical diagnosis. However, this type of hearsay testimony can only be used to prove the accuracy of the doctor's diagnosis and not make the doctor a vehicle for his patient to take the stand. A doctor's hearsay testimony which is irrelevant or not helpful to making a diagnosis will not be admitted under this hearsay exception.

NOTES:

MEANY v. UNITED STATES

112 F.2d 538 (1940)

NATURE OF CASE: **Appeal of adverse judgment by plaintiff.**

FACT SUMMARY: **Not stated in casebook excerpt.**

CONCISE RULE OF LAW: **When a person gives his present and past medical history to a doctor solely for the purpose of promoting effective treatment, the doctor can testify to those statements both in support of his diagnosis and to their own intrinsic truth.**

FACTS: Not stated in casebook excerpt.

ISSUE: May statements made by a patient to his physician for diagnostic purposes by testified to by the physician and be used as evidence of facts?

HOLDING AND DECISION: (J. L. Hand) Yes. Testimony of a patient's statements describing his past medical history and condition made to aid in diagnosis by a doctor is different from excited outcries a patient may make to his doctor. The spontineity and lack of any opportunity for reflection by the declarant makes these spontaneous utterances trustworthy and an admissible exception to the hearsay rule. Statements of past medical history and present medical condition are made by patients trying to be as honest as possible in order to promote their own recovery by ensuring an accurate diagnosis and effective treatment. This is also quite different from facts stated by a patient that are irrelevant to the patient's treatment, such as causes of the injury observed by the patient. A patient has less of a self-interested motive to pinpoint blame than to describe symptoms or past diagnosis to a doctor. The jury is still free to weigh the credibility of the doctor's testimony, but a court cannot logically deny a presumption of truthfulness when the hearsay declarant's self-preservation forces him to be honest. Reversed; new trial ordered.

EDITOR'S ANALYSIS: The hearsay exception allowing a doctor to testify about his or her patient's statements made in the course of diagnosis is extended from being admitted to prove the accuracy of the diagnosis to proving the facts they conain.

NOTES:

MUTUAL LIFE INSURANCE CO. v. HILLMAN

SUPREME COURT OF THE UNITED STATES,
1892. 145 U.S. 285, 12 S. Ct. 909

NATURE OF CASE: Action to recover on a life insurance policy.

FACTUAL SUMMARY: Where the issue at trial was whether a body found at a creek was Hillman, so as to establish his death and thus enable his widow (P) to collect under a life insurance policy, Mutual Life Insurance Co. (D) sought to introduce letters sent by Walters to his fiancee and sister which stated Walters' intention to accompany Hillman.

CONCISE RULE OF LAW: Declarations of state of mind which tend to evince a plan or intent to perform an act may be introduced into evidence as proof that the act has, in fact, been committed.

FACTS: Hillman had a life insurance policy, issued by Mutual Life Insurance Co. (D), naming his widow (P) as beneficiary. When Hillman disappeared, his widow (P) brought an action to collect under the policy. The widow (P) introduced evidence that Hillman had left Wichita on or about March 5, 1879, and that on March 18, he was accidentally killed at a creek. The insurance company (D) introduced evidence which suggested that the body found at the creek was one Walters, and not Hillman. To substantiate this claim, the insurance company (P) sought to introduce letters written by Walters to his fiancee and sister in which Walters, just before March 5, expressed his intention of leaving Wichita with Hillman. Apparently, Walters was also missing and the body found at the creek was unidentifiable. The trial judge refused to admit the letters into evidence.

ISSUE: Are out-of-court statements which tend to prove the intention of the declarant at a particular moment in time admissible?

HOLDING AND DECISION: Yes. When the intention to be proved is important only as qualifying an act, its connection with that act must be shown in order to warrant the admission of declarations of the intention. But whenever the intention is, of itself, a distinct and material fact in a chain of circumstances, it may be proved by contemporaneous oral or written declarations of the party. Especially where the declarant is, or believed, dead, there can hardly be any other way of proving his intention. Even when alive, his memory is probably less trustworthy than letters written by him at the very time and under circumstances precluding a suspicion of misrepresentation. The letters in question were competent, not as narratives of facts, nor as proof that Hillman had actually left Wichita, but that he had the intention of doing so, which made it more probable that he, in fact, did leave.

EDITOR'S ANALYSIS: Questionable sincerity, and remoteness in time, of course, act as limitations on the admissibility of a declarant's past intentions in order to prove the commission of some act by the declarant. Some commentators have suggested two further limitations to the rule given in this case: (1) such evidence should only be admitted when the declarant himself is unable to testify; (2) declarations used to establish subsequent conduct should not be admitted when the plan expressed by the intention required the cooperation of another person. The reason for this latter limitation is that the chances of carrying out the plan are reduced where another person is involved.

NOTES:

SHEPARD v. UNITED STATES

290 U.S. 96 (1933)

NATURE OF CASE: **Appeal of conviction for murder.**

FACT SUMMARY: **Shepard (D) challenged the Court of Appeals ruling that certain statements made by his wife were admissible as declarations of state of mind.**

CONCISE RULE OF LAW: **Declarations of state of mind are admissible only to prove a present state of mind, and not as proof of prior acts committed by someone else.**

FACTS: At Shepard's (D) trial for murdering his wife, several witnesses testified on his behalf as to the presence of a suicidal intent or inclination in his wife's mind. The Court of Appeals found that certain statements made by Mrs. Shepard as to her belief that Shepard (D) had poisoned her were admissible as declarations of her state of mind. The Court of Appeals affirmed Shepard's (D) earlier conviction for murder, and he filed a writ of certiorari.

ISSUE: Can declarations of a person's state of mind be offered as proof of prior acts committed by someone else?

HOLDING AND DECISION: (Cardozo, J.) No. Declarations of a state of mind are admissible only to prove a present state of mind and not as proof of prior acts committed by someone else. There are times when a state of mind, if relevant, may be proved by contemporaneous declarations of feeling or intent. When a criminal defendant introduces the issue, declarations as to state of mind are admissible for rebuttal purposes. But the declarations can ony be used to show present state of mind, and not for other purposes. Here, Shepard (D) introduced the issue by raising questions as to suicidal intent present in the mind of his wife. Shepard (D) would have had no grievance had the prosecution merely used the statement for rebuttal. The prosecution offered this as evidence that she was dying of poison given to her by her husband. To expect the jury to consider this evidence only with respect to Mrs. Shepard's will to live and to disregard it to the extent that she was dying at Shepard's (D) hands is unreasonable. Where confusion of this sort is presented, evidence should be excluded. Reversed and remanded.

EDITOR'S ANALYSIS: This "blanket exclusion of statements of memory or belief to prove past events" has remained relatively intact despite substantial reexamination. (McCormick on Evidence, 3rd Ed. pg. 852). This prohibition remains in effect in the Federal Rules except as to wills, where the statement will be admitted if related to the "execution, revocation, identification or terms of the declarant's will." See Fed. R. Evid. 803(3).

NOTES:

PALMER v. HOFFMAN

UNITED STATES SUPREME COURT, 1943.
318 U.S. 109, 63 S. Ct. 477

NATURE OF CASE: Action for personal injuries arising out of a railroad accident.

FACT SUMMARY: The engineer of a train involved in an accident, who died before trial, made a statement to the railroad company regarding the accident. This statement was not allowed in evidence.

CONCISE RULE OF LAW: A business record, to be in the regular course of business, must be made in relation to the inherent nature of the business, and in the methods systematically employed for the conduct of the business as a business.

FACTS: Palmer (P) was injured in an accident with a railroad train, and brought suit against Hoffman (D), a trustee of the railroad. Shortly after the accident, the engineer of the train made a statement to the superintendent of the railroad and to a representative of the public utilities commission. It was the custom of the railroad to record such statements whenever there was an accident. The engineer died before the trial, and Hoffman (D) attempted to introduce the statement into evidence. A statute allowed business records to be admitted if made in the course of regular business, but the court would not allow it into evidence.

ISSUE: Was the accident report made in the regular course of business?

HOLDING AND DECISION: No. To be considered made in the regular course of business, a record must be made in relation to the inherent nature of the business, and in the methods systematically employed for the conduct of the business as a business. The keeping of accident reports, while customary, is not essential to the efficient operation of a railroad. If the mere custom of making a record of non-essential activity could bring that record within the meaning of "regular course" of business, then any company could bring any type of record into court. The primary purpose of the record in this case was not for the efficient management of a railroad, but it was for litigation. Therefore, the record was not within the regular course of business, and thereby was properly excluded.

EDITOR'S ANALYSIS: This case is the leading case on what is the regular course of business. Many scholars have criticized the decision as being contrary to the statute, and therefore many lower courts have dealt with the case in varying ways. The accepted analysis of this case today is that it does not create a blanket rule of exclusion for "self serving" accident reports or other such records kept by businesses. Rather, it has been construed as creating a discretionary power in the trial court to exclude evidence which may fall within the requirements of the business records exception to the hearsay rule, but under the circumstances appears to lack the trustworthiness which ordinary businesses are deemed to have. The motive and the opportunity to falsify are the primary factors in using this case to exclude records.

JOHNSON v. LUTZ

COURT OF APPEALS OF NEW YORK, 1930.
253 N.Y. 124, 170 N.E. 517

NATURE OF CASE: Wrongful death action based on a traffic accident.

FACT SUMMARY: Lutz (D) attempted to get an accident report filed by a policeman into evidence. The report contained statements of witnesses to the traffic accident.

CONCISE RULE OF LAW: Even if a statute allows business records to be admitted without first-hand knowledge of the recorder if done in the regular course of business, this does not include entries that include hearsay statements of third parties not engaged in the business related to the record.

FACTS: Johnson (P) was killed in a traffic accident with Lutz (D). In order to prove that he was not at fault, Lutz (D) attempted to have an accident report admitted into evidence. The report was made by a police officer on duty, and included statements of witnesses to the accident. A statute in effect provided that records kept in the normal course of business are admissible without the first-hand knowledge of the recorder. However, the court did not allow the report into evidence.

ISSUE: Does the statute extend to allow records that include statements of persons not engaged in the business into evidence?

HOLDING AND DECISION: No. Even if a statute allows records made in the course of business to be admitted without first-hand knowledge, this does not extend to records that include statements of third parties that are not engaged in the business related to the record. The purpose of the statute was to allow proof of business transactions without the necessity of calling all the parties involved in situations involving normal business conditions. The essence of this statute was to provide credence to records made by persons in the exercise of the business duty. The intent of the legislature was not to extend this rule to statements made by persons outside the business for which the report was made, such as witnesses to an accident. Therefore, the report was properly excluded.

EDITOR'S ANALYSIS: The statute in question in this case was passed to remedy situations such as the one that existed in the previous case. Had this statute been in effect in that case, as it would have been in most jurisdictions today, the shopbook would have been admissible to prove the account receivable. However, as this case indicates, to apply this type of statute to a record, not only must the recorder be under a business duty to record the information, but the persons giving him the information must be under a similar duty. In other words, it's not enough that the policeman was under a business duty to make the report in this case, but the witnesses must have also been under a business duty in reporting to the police. Obviously, they were not under such a duty and, therefore, the report was not admissible. This rule has been severely criticized, but still stands as the majority rule.

UNITED STATES v. OATES

U.S.Ct. of Appls., 2nd Cir.,1977. 560 F.2d 45

NATURE OF CASE: Appeal from a conviction for drug-related offenses.

FACT SUMMARY: Oates (D) claimed that the chemist's report and worksheet identifying the substance seized from him as heroin should have been excluded from evidence as hearsay.

CONCISE RULE OF LAW: Evaluative and law enforcement reports which fail to qualify under the "public records" exception to the hearsay rule cannot be admitted as "business."

FACTS: Oates (D) was convicted of possession of heroin with intent to distribute and conspiracy to commit that substantive offense. On appeal he charged the trial judge erred in admitting into evidence the official report and worksheet of a U.S. Customs Service chemist identifying the substance seized from Oates (D) as heroin. The chemist who wrote the documents was "unavailable," so the Government (P) called another Customs Service chemist to testify to the regular procedures and practices used by Customs Service chemists in analyzing unknown substances. She claimed to be able to ascertain from the worksheet the various steps the other chemist had used to determine if the substance was heroin. When Oates (D) made a convincing argument that such documents were not admissible under Federal Rule of Evidence 803(8)'s "public records" exception to the hearsay rule, the Government (P) claimed they were nonetheless admissible under the "business records" exception of Rule 803(6).

ISSUE: Are evaluative and law enforcement reports admissible as "business records"?

HOLDING AND DECISION: No. In passing the Federal Rules of Evidence, Congress made clear its intent that evaluative and law enforcement reports be absolutely inadmissible against defendants in criminal cases. So, letting them in as "business records" when they are explicitly precluded from coming in under the more fitting "public records" exception is improper. F.R.E. 803(8)(C) specifically states that "factual findings resulting from an investigation made pursuant to authority granted by law" are not shielded from the exclusionary effect of the hearsay rule by the "public records" exception if the Government seeks to admit them against the accused in a criminal trial. F.R.E. 803(8)(B) creates a "public records" exception that specifically excludes "matters observed by police officers and other law enforcement personnel" (which means any officer or employee of a governmental agency which has law enforcement responsibilities). The documents introduced at trial in this case should thus not have been admitted. Reversed and remanded for a new trial.

EDITOR'S ANALYSIS: Fear that interference with the accused's right to confrontation would lead Congress to conclude that evaluative and law enforcement reports should not be admissible against a criminal defendant under any exception to the hearsay rule. However, they can be used in civil cases and proceedings and against the Government in criminal cases, unless they are untrustworthy.

DALLAS CNTY. v. COMMERCIAL UNION ASSUR.CO., LTD.

U.S. CT.OF APP., 5th Cir., 1961. 286 F.2d 388

NATURE OF CASE: Action to collect under insurance policy.

FACT SUMMARY: Insurer (D) offered into evidence a 1901 newspaper article.

CONCISE RULE OF LAW: In matters of local interest, when the fact in question is of such a public nature it would be generally known throughout the community, and when the questioned fact occurred so long ago that the testimony of an eye witness would probably be less trustworthy than a contemporary newspaper account, a federal court may relax the hearsay exclusionary rules to the extent of admitting the newspaper article in evidence.

FACTS: In 1957, the Dallas County (P) court house collapsed. In order to collect under an insurance policy which covered loss caused by lightning, the County (P) reported the presence of charcoal and charred timbers found in the building's ruins. To refute this at trial, the insurer (D), claiming that the charred remains were present in the building prior to its collapse, offered into evidence a local 1901 newspaper article, unsigned, which reported a fire in the court house. The County (P) objected to the introduction of the article on the ground of hearsay.

ISSUE: May a federal court ever admit into evidence a newspaper article?

HOLDING AND DECISION: Yes. F.R.C.P. 43(a) permits a federal court to follow any rule which favors the reception of evidence. Although nearly all newspaper articles constitute hearsay, a federal court may recognize its own exceptions. First, it is due to necessity that the article should be admitted. Witnesses to the 1901 fire would now either be dead or possess a faulty memory. Secondly, the article itself carries sufficient indicia of trustworthiness. A small town newspaper reporter in 1901 would not report a local fire unless there had, in fact, been one. The reporter would simply lack any motive to falsify. The article is admissible in evidence.

EDITOR'S ANALYSIS: Newspaper articles, printed books or publications are usually not admissible in evidence. This is because, absent some special indication of reliability, as in the instant case, there is no opportunity to cross-examine their authors, and the statements within were not made under oath.

NOTES:

UNITED STATES v. BAILEY

439 F. Supp. 1303 (W.D.Pa. 1977)

NATURE OF CASE: Motion for new trial or acquittal from armed robbery conviction.

FACT SUMMARY: The written confession of a co-conspirator made after the robbery was allowed into evidence against Bailey (D) when the co-conspirator refused to testify against Bailey (D) at Bailey's (D) trial in an attempt to prevent Bailey's (D) conviction.

CONCISE RULE OF LAW: Hearsay evidence admitted under a residual hearsay exception (Federal Rules of Evidence, Rule 804(b)(5)) must also satisfy requirements imposed by the Confrontation Clause of the Sixth Amendment of the United States Constitution.

FACTS: Bailey (D) and Stewart robbed a bank. Stewart was identified from palm prints left on a bank counter and made a written confession implicating Bailey (D) in order to plea bargain for a lesser sentence. At Bailey's (D) trial, Stewart refused to testify against Bailey (D) in order to prevent Bailey (D) from being convicted. The government (P), instead, introduced Stewart's written confession by reading it into the record. Bailey (D) was only able to cross-examine by impeaching the credibility of Stewart's written confession on the basis of Stewart's previous criminal record. Bailey (D) moved for a new trial and/or acquittal after being convicted.

ISSUE: Must hearsay evidence admitted under the residual hearsay exception also satisfy requirements imposed by the Sixth Amendment's Confrontation Clause?

HOLDING AND DECISION: (J. Teitelbaum) Yes. The residual exception to the hearsay rule and the Confrontation Clause of the Sixth Amendment are separate limits to the admission of evidence. Hearsay evidence which meets the requirements of the residual hearsay exception (listed on Rule 804(6)(5))may still be disallowed because it violates protections guaranteed by the Sixth Amendment. The only way that Bailey (D) could have refuted Stewart's confession in a cross-examination was to impeach Stewart's credibility with Stewart's prior convictions. Any stronger attempt to confront Stewart directly would have strengthened the government's (P) case against Bailey (D) giving Stewart a chance to bring out more details of the robbery in a cross-examination than the government (P) had already presented in the written confession. This was why Stewart felt that he could help Bailey (D), his friend, by refusing to testify. Since Bailey (D) could not have been helped by more Sixth Amendment protection than he had received, Bailey (D) was not prejudiced by not receiving the extra protections he might have received in a different situation. Rule 804(b)(5) requirements were satisfied because: (1), the statement was offered to prove identity, a material fact; (2), the statement was more probative for identity than any other reasonably possible evidence; (3), the general purpose of the Rules of Evidence of guaranteeing the trustworthiness of evidence while ensuring that justice is done is best served by admitting Stewart's statement; (4), the failure of pretrial disclosure of the evidence was not the government's (P) fault, and Bailey (D) was given a sufficient recess to contest admittance of the statement; (5), the hearsay declarant, Stewart, had made himself unavailable to testify; and (6), the statement had circumstantial guarantees of trustworthiness.

EDITOR'S ANALYSIS: Rule 804(b)(5), discussed above, and Rule 803(24) are the two residual exceptions to the hearsay rule in the Federal Rules of Evidence. Residual exceptions are given a very narrow focus and must meet difficult foundational and Constitutional requirements because of their potential for giving a judge discretion broad enough to eliminate the rule against hearsay evidence. Bailey (D) also appealed the above holding and finally succeeded in having Stewart's statement thrown out and in being acquitted. The two lower courts failed to consider that Stewart's statement violated the general purpose of trustworthiness in the evidence rules. Stewart's statement could have been in Stewart's interest at the time it was made. Since Stewart had already admitted guilt in a plea bargain, another confession could not hurt him. Stewart might have used the confession to put the blame on Bailey (D) so as to cover up for his real partner in the robbery. Thus, Stewart's statement could not be assumed to be trustworthy, expecially without any cross-examination to check it.

NOTES:

UNITED STATES v. WEST

U.S. Ct. of Appls., 4th Cir.,1978. 574 F.2d 1131

NATURE OF CASE: Appeal from conviction for distributing and possessing heroin.

FACT SUMMARY: West (D) argued that the grand jury testimony of Brown, who was slain prior to trial, should not have been admitted under the "residual" exception to the hearsay rule because it lacked the requisite guarantees of trustworthiness due to Brown's criminal record and unavailability.

CONCISE RULE OF LAW: A statement is admissible under the "residual" exception to the hearsay rule in the Federal Rules of Evidence if there are circumstantial guarantees of its trustworthiness equivalent to those justifying any one of the specific exceptions to the hearsay rule.

FACTS: Brown testified before a grand jury concerning the drug transactions he set up under strict surveillance and monitoring while working voluntarily with drug authorities while in prison on a drug charge. West (D) appealed his drug conviction, charging that the grand jury testimony of Brown, who died before his trial, should not have been admitted under Fed. Rule of Evid. 804(b)(5), which provides a residual exception to the hearsay rule for statements not falling within specific exceptions to the hearsay rule but having equivalent circumstantial guarantees of trustworthiness. West (D) argued Brown's criminal past and unavailability for cross-examination prevented this equivalency requirement from being met. The Government (P) urged that the equivalency requirement was and is met whenever the circumstantial guarantees of trustworthiness are at least equal to those justifying any one of the several specific exceptions to the hearsay rule.

ISSUE: Must there be circumstantial guarantees of a statement's trustworthiness equivalent to those justifying any one of the specific exceptions to the hearsay rule for it to be admitted under the "residual" exception to the hearsay rule found in the Federal Rules of Evidence?

HOLDING AND DECISION: Yes. A prerequisite to admission of a statement under the "residual" exception to the hearsay rule is that there be "equivalent" circumstantial guarantees of its trustworthiness. This means there must be guarantees of trustworthiness equivalent to those justifying any one of the specific exceptions to the hearsay rule. Here, the corroborative circumstances and verification procedures lent to Brown's grand jury testimony a degree of trustworthiness probably substantially exceeding that inherent in dying declarations, statements against interest, and statements of personal or family history. Thus, the aforementioned requirement is met. Affirmed.

EDITOR'S ANALYSIS: The residual hearsay exception in the Federal Rules of Evidence had a stormy legislative history. The House of Representatives deleted the initial draft, which the Senate later reinstated in a narrower form. Finally, it was passed by a compromise in which a notice provision was added.

UNITED STATES v. GARNER

U.S. Ct. of Apls., 4th Cir., 1978, 574 F.2d 1141

NATURE OF CASE: Appeal from convictions for drug related offenses.

FACT SUMMARY: The trial court had admitted into evidence the sworn grand jury testimony of an alleged coconspirator who refused to testify fully at Garner's (D) trial.

CONCISE RULE OF LAW: It does not constitute a violation of the Confrontation Clause of the Constitution to admit into evidence at a criminal trial the sworn grand jury testimony of one unavailable as a witness (under the residual hearsay exception) as long as such testimony bears sufficient guarantees of reliability and the circumstances contain a sufficient basis upon which the jury may assess its trustworthiness.

FACTS: Before the grand jury, Robinson had testified fully concerning a heroin importing scheme in which he participated with Garner (D). At Garner's (D) trial, however, he initially refused to testify. Eventually, after being given use immunity and threatened with contempt, Robinson said he might answer questions, but only those put to him by defense counsel. So, he was declared "unavailable" as a witness and his grand jury testimony was admitted into evidence under the residual hearsay exception. On appeal, Garner (D) complained that this was a violation of the Confrontation Clause of the Constitution.

ISSUE: In a criminal trial, can the sworn grand jury testimony of an unavailable witness be admitted into evidence without violating the Confrontation Clause of the Constitution?

HOLDING AND DECISION: (C.J. Haynsworth) Yes. Sworn grand jury testimony may be admitted under the residual hearsay exception (found in Rule 804(b)(5) of the Federal Rules of Evidence) when there are substantial guarantees of trustworthiness equivalent to those which warrant recognized exceptions to the hearsay rule. The admission of such sworn testimony is not a violation of the Confrontation Clause of the Constitution if it bears sufficient guarantees of reliability and the circumstances contain a sufficient basis upon which the jury may assess its trustworthiness. In this particular case, there are strong indicators of reliability and the jury had an ample basis upon which to determine the trustworthiness of the testimony. Other evidence and testimony corroborated the account Robinson gave in his grand jury testimony. It was testimony that was properly admitted at trial. Affirmed.

DISSENT: (C.J. Widender) I dissent to admitting the grand jury testimony for the reasons I have expressed in United States v. Payne, 492 F.2d 449 and United States v. West, 574 F.2d 1131.

EDITOR'S ANALYSIS: Grand jury testimony was admitted in United States v. Thevis, 665 F.2d 616 (5th Cir. 1982), but under a "waiver" theory which is based on the notion that a defendant whose own conduct (such as making threats) makes the declarant "unavailable" to testify effectively "waives" his right to confrontation.

MATTOX v. UNITED STATES

156 U.S. 237 (1895)

NATURE OF CASE: Appeal from conviction for murder.

FACT SUMMARY: The government (P) offered transcripts from the first trial of testimony of key witnesses who died before the new trial, and Mattox (D) argued that admission of this evidence was a denial of his Sixth Amendment right to confront witnesses.

CONCISE RULE OF LAW: The prior testimony exception to the rule against hearsay evidence does not violate the Sixth Amendment right to confront witnesses.

FACTS: Mattox (P) had been convicted of murder. This first conviction was reversed and a new trial ordered. In the time between the two trials, the two key witnesses against Mattox (P) died. At the new trial, the court admitted transcripts of the deceased witnesses' testimony. Mattox (P) appealed his conviction at the new trial because he was denied a chance to confront and cross-examine these witnesses.

ISSUE: In a criminal case, is there an exception to the rule against hearsay allowing into evidence the transcripts of testimony taken and cross-examined in a previous trial even though the defendant has no opportunity to confront the witnesses in the second trial?

HOLDING AND DECISION: (J. Brown) Yes. Constitutional protections are not absolute. While exceptions to Constitutional protections are more reluctantly allowed for criminal cases than for civil cases, a balance between protecting a defendant from untrustworthy evidence and protecting the public from unpunished criminals must be struck. Here, the opportunity for Mattox (P) to cross-examine the witnesses at the first trial makes this right less important at a re-trial of the case.

EDITOR'S ANALYSIS: While the demeanor of the witness and the chance to question a witness about inconsistencies are crucial for credibility, testimony without these checks is not necessarily untrustworthy as long as there are other credibility checks. Spontaneity, for example, is a credibility check for the hearsay of spontaneous or excital utterances. Here, a previous opportunity for cross-examination is a sufficient credibility to allow an exception to the Sixth Amendment while upholding its spirit requiring credible evidence.

NOTES:

KIRBY v. UNITED STATES

174 U.S. 47 (1899)

NATURE OF CASE: **Appeal from conviction for receiving stolen property.**

FACT SUMMARY: **The government (P) won a conviction of Kirby (D) merely by introducing conviction records of the three thieves convicted of stealing the property found in Kirby's (D) possession to show that the property belonged to the federal government (P).**

CONCISE RULE OF LAW: **A defendant in a criminal case must be able to confront the witnesses testifying against him under the Sixth Amendment of the U.S. Constitution.**

FACTS: Three thieves of federal property were either found guilty or confessed to their crime. In order to convict Kirby (D) of receiving stolen government (P) property, the government (P) introduced only the records of the three thieves to show that the property was indeed stolen government (P) property. Kirby (D) appealed the denial of any chance to cross-examine the thieves either at their confessions or at his own trial, and the denial of any chance to cross-examine witnesses against the thieves.

ISSUE: Can a defendant be denied all rights to confront adverse witnesses in a criminal trial?

HOLDING AND DECISION: (J. Harlan) No. In order for the government (P) to convict Kirby (D) of receiving stolen federal property, the government (P) must first show that the principal thief was convicted before any receiver (such as Kirby (D)) of stolen goods may be punished, and that the property in Kirby's possession was in fact federal property. The record of the thieves' convictions can be used to show the former, but not the latter. The source of the property goes to prove the crime itself allegedly committed by Kirby (D). Kirby (D) must be given an opportunity to confront evidence used to prove a crime against him under the Sixth Amendment.

EDITOR'S ANALYSIS: The deciding factor in this case was that there was no check of any kind on the credibility of the evidence used against Kirby (D). If the government (P) had compelled one or more of the three thieves to testify at Kirby's (D) trial that Kirby (D) had received the stolen property, Kirby (D) might have been convicted.

NOTES:

POINTER v. STATE OF TEXAS

SUP. CT. OF U.S., 1965. 380 U.S. 400, 85 S. Ct. 1065

NATURE OF CASE: Appeal from a robbery conviction.

NOTES:

FACT SUMMARY: Because a prosecution witness was unavailable at the trial, the prosecution introduced a transcript of the witness's testimony at the preliminary hearing. At the preliminary hearing, Pointer (D) did not have an attorney, nor did he have the right to one.

CONCISE RULE OF LAW: A transcript of prior testimony offered against a criminal defendant violates the Sixth Amendment right of confrontation if the prior testimony is taken at a time, and under such circumstances, that the defendant, through counsel, was not afforded an adequate opportunity of cross-examination.

FACTS: Pointer (D) was arrested for robbing Phillips. At the preliminary hearing, Phillips identified Pointer (D). At that hearing, Pointer (D) was without counsel, and was bound over for trial. At the trial, Phillips, having moved, was not available to testify. The prosecution was then allowed to introduce the transcript with his preliminary hearing testimony into evidence.

ISSUE: Did the use of the transcript of the preliminary hearing violate Pointer's (D) Sixth Amendment right to confront witnesses against him?

HOLDING AND DECISION: Yes. A transcript of prior testimony offered against a criminal defendant violates the Sixth Amendment right of confrontation if the prior testimony is taken at a time, and under such circumstances that the defendant, through counsel, was not offered an adequate opportunity of cross-examination. While the Sixth Amendment only applies to the Federal Courts, the right of adequate cross-examination is one of the safeguards that is essential to a fair trial. Therefore, it is such a fundamental right that it is to be applied to the State Courts under the due process clause of the Fourteenth Amendment. The fact that Pointer (D) was present at the preliminary hearing and could have cross-examined Phillips is immaterial, for, to have an adequate opportunity, there must be the presence of counsel. Without a right to counsel, there is no real cross-examination.

CONCURRENCE: There was no adequate cross-examination, however, the Sixth Amendment is not a fundamental guarantee under due process.

EDITOR'S ANASYSIS: Actual cross-examination is not required for the prior testimony exceptions to the hearsay rule. All that is necessary is that there was an adequate and reasonable opportunity that was offered and either accepted or waived. As this case indicates, testimony given at a preliminary hearing has created problems for the courts. Where there was no counsel present, as in this case, there are constitutional problems, but even if counsel is present there still may be complications. Many times in preliminary hearings, counsel will not cross-examine a witness for strategic reasons. An argument has been made that, therefore, there was no adequate right of cross-examination. This argument has not been received favorably by the courts.

DOUGLAS v. ALABAMA

380 U.S. 415 (1965)

NATURE OF CASE: Appeal from conviction for murder.

FACT SUMMARY: The government (P) read into evidence the confession of Douglas' (D) co-conspirator as an impeachment document to the co-conspirator's act of pleading the Fifth Amendment on the stand, and Douglas (D) was unable to cross-examine the co-conspirator as a result.

CONCISE RULE OF LAW: A criminal defendant has a constitutional right to confront all witnesses testifying against him.

FACTS: Douglas' (D) co-conspirator, Loyd, had been convicted prior to Douglas (D). Because Loyd planned to appeal his conviction, Loyd pleaded the Fifth Amendment while testifying against Douglas (D) at Douglas' trial. The government (P) impeached Loyd's "testimony" by reading a detailed confession allegedly written by Loyd. Loyd continued to plead the Fifth. Douglas (D) was thereby effectively denied any opportunity to cross-examine Loyd about the details of his confession and appealed the conviction resulting from it.

ISSUE: Does the lack of an opportunity to cross-examine a witness constitute a violation of the Sixth Amendment's confrontation clause?

HOLDING AND DECISION: (J. Brennan) Yes. The lack of an opportunity to cross-examine constitutes a violation of the Sixth Amendment. The reading of the confession could have been easily equated by a jury to the testimony of Loyd and believed as such. This belief cannot be allowed to stand without first being tested for credibility by the defendant through cross-examination. Since Douglas (D) could not cross-examine Loyd who was pleading the Fifth and a cross-examination of the prosecutor would be insufficient with regard to inconsistencies of detail in the confession itself, Douglas (D) had no real opportunity to cross-examine or confront the witness.

EDITOR'S ANALYSIS: A jury or trier of fact is not be allowed to believe evidence that does not have some substantial check or test of the credibility or believability of the evidence. This is the key policy behind the rule against hearsay and its exceptions and the protection afforded by the confrontation clause of the Sixth Amendment.

NOTES:

BARBER v. PAGE

SUP. CT. OF THE U.S., 1968. 390 U.S. 719, 88 S. Ct. 1318

NATURE OF CASE: Appeal from the denial of a writ of habeas corpus based on a robbery conviction.

FACT SUMMARY: A witness against Barber (D) at the preliminary hearing was in prison in another State at the time of trial. The State was allowed to use his preliminary hearing testimony without showing any attempt to subpoena him.

CONCISE RULE OF LAW: A witness is not unavailable for the purposes of the prior testimony exception to the right of confrontation unless the prosecutorial authorities have made a good-faith effort to obtain his presence at trial.

FACTS: Barber (D) and Woods were jointly charged with robbery. At the preliminary hearing, Woods gave testimony which incriminated Barber (D). At the time of trial, Woods was in prison in another State. The prosecution, without making any effort to obtain Woods' presence, was allowed to introduce into evidence the transcript of his testimony at the preliminary hearing.

ISSUE: Is it necessary to make an effort to obtain the presence of an unavailable witness before using his prior testimony?

HOLDING AND DECISION: Yes. A witness is not unavailable for the purposes of the prior testimony exception to the right of confrontation unless the prosecutorial authorities have made a good-faith attempt to obtain his presence at trial. It is very possible that if the prosecution had attempted, they could have obtained Woods' presence at the trial. There has been an increasing amount of cooperation between jurisdictions, and it is generally the policy to allow prisoners to testify in other State Courts. The Sixth Amendment right of confrontation is a fundamental right, and is, therefore, applied to the States through the Fourteenth Amendment. It appears here that the sole reason that Barber (D) could not confront Woods was that the State did not attempt to seek his presence. The right of confrontation may not be dispensed with so lightly.

EDITOR'S ANALYSIS: What exactly renders a witness unavailable has been in a constant mode of change. At common law, the only acceptable showing of unavailability was when the witness was dead. This was expanded through witnesses that could not be found after the exercise of due diligence to those who were permanently or indefinitely outside the jurisdiction. Prior to this case, many jurisdictions had extended the rule in both civil and criminal cases to a witness that was temporarily out of the jurisdiction. It should be noted that such a rule would still be constitutional without a showing of an effort to obtain the witness in civil cases, even after this decision. However, many courts now require, even in a civil case, that it is shown that the witness cannot be induced to voluntarily return and testify. This civil rule is only statutory, however, and does not have its origin in the constitution.

NOTES:

BRUTON v. UNITED STATES

391 U.S. 123 (1968)

NATURE OF CASE: Appeal from conviction for armed postal robbery.

FACT SUMMARY: Bruton (D) appealed his conviction for armed postal robbery, urging that it should be set aside since at his joint trial a co-defendant's confession inculpating Bruton had been admitted.

CONCISE RULE OF LAW: Where defendants are tried jointly, the admission of a co-defendant's confession that inculpates the other defendant deprives the other defendant of the right to confront the witness against him, even in the presence of a limiting jury instruction.

FACTS: Bruton (D) and Evans were each convicted in a joint trial of armed postal robbery. A postal inspector had obtained oral confessions from Evans inculpating both men in the robbery while Evans was in custody. The trial judge instructed the jury that the oral confessions were competant evidence against Evans but was inadmissable hearsay against Bruton's (D) guilt or innocence. Both men appealed. Evan's conviction was set aside on the grounds that the confessions were improperly received, but since the jury was instructed to disregard them as to Bruton (D), his conviction was affirmed. Bruton (D) then appealed.

ISSUE: Where defendant's are tried jointly, does the admission of a co-defendant's confession that inculpates the other defendant deprive the other defendant of the right to confront the witnesses against him, even in the presence of a limiting jury instruction?

HOLDING AND DECISION: (Brennan, J.) Yes. Where defendants are tried jointly, the admission of a co-defendant's confession that inculpates the other defendant deprives the other defendant of the right to confront the witnesses against him, even in the presence of a limiting jury instruction. Precedent assumed that encroachment on the right to confrontation could be avoided by instruction to the jury to disregard by the line of cases requiring evidentiary hearings on the issue of voluntariness of confessions. Where as here, there is substantial risk that the jury looked to the improper evidence to determine Bruton's (D) guilt, admission of this confession denied Bruton (D) his constitutional right to confront the witnesses against him. Reversed.

DISSENT: (White, J.) Just as a jury can be reasonably expected to ignore ordinary hearsay or other inadmissible evidence when instructed to do so, so should a jury be able to disregard the portions of a co-defendant's confession implicating the defendant when instructed to do so.

EDITOR'S ANALYSIS: This is a departure from the general practice to admit the evidence with limiting instructions. It has been held, however, that where the other evidence against a defendant is so strong that a co-defendant's confession admitted was harmless beyond a reasonable doubt, reversal will not be required. See Harrington v. California, 395 U.S. 250 (1969).

NOTES:

HARRINGTON v. CALIFORNIA
395 U.S. 250 (1969)

NATURE OF CASE: **Appeal from conviction for felony murder in course of attempted armed robbery.**

FACT SUMMARY: **Confessions of two non-testifying co-defendants were admitted in a joint trial involving Harrington (D) after the admittance of the more incriminating confession of a third co-defendant who testified and was cross-examined.**

CONCISE RULE OF LAW: **Confessions of non-testifying co-defendants are not erroneously or prejudicially admitted if more incriminating evidence than the evidence contained in the confessions has already been properly admitted and is itself strong enough to convict the defendant without considering the confessions of non-testifying co-defendants.**

FACTS: Harrington (D), a white man, who was charged under the felony-murder rule, and Bosby, Rhone, and Cooper, black men, attempted to rob a store. All four fled after Bosby shot a store clerk. Bosby and Cooper confessed that a white man was there with them, but did not testify at the joint trial of the four. Harrington (D) confessed that he was at the store at the time of the attempted robbery and fled with the other three. Rhone testified about his confession placing Harrington (D) in the store with a gun at the time and was cross-examined by Harrington (D). Harrington (D) appealed his conviction as being based in part on Bosby's and Cooper's confessions which he had no opportunity to test with cross-examination.

ISSUE: If the evidence properly admitted against a defendant is non-circumstantial and strong enough alone to convict defendant, is it prejudicial error to admit less incriminating evidence that is not tested by a Sixth Amendment cross-examination confronting the evidence?

HOLDING AND DECISION: (J. Douglas) No. If evidence admitted without the protection of cross-examination can do no more harm to Harrington's (D) case than the evidence already in the record, it is not prejudicial error to have admitted the weaker evidence without allowing it to be cross-examined. Based on the special facts of the case, the properly admitted evidence contained in Rhone's testimony and Harrington's (D) own confession was strong enough alone to convict Harrington (D). The confessions of the other co-defendants incriminated Harrington (D) too weakly to have any significant prejudicial effect and constituted harmless error beyond a reasonable doubt. Harrington (D) could not have gained much by cross-examining Bosby and Cooper about their confessions.

EDITOR'S ANALYSIS: Some constitutional rights are so fundamental to a fair trial that any infraction of them is reversible error. The right to confront witnesses under the Sixth Amendment is not so absolutely fundamental. Certain limited exceptions are tolerated by the court.

NOTES:

CALIFORNIA v. GREEN

399 U.S. 149 (1970)

NATURE OF CASE: Appeal from a conviction of supplying marijuana to a minor.

FACT SUMMARY: Porter identified Green (D) as the supplier of his marijuana.

CONCISE RULE OF LAW: Testimony of a witness at a preliminary hearing subject to full cross-examination at that time may be introduced as substantive evidence or as prior inconsistent statements.

FACTS: Porter, a minor, was charged with selling marijuana. Porter implicated Green (D) as his supplier. Green (D) was arrested and charged with supplying marijuana to a minor. At the preliminary hearing, Porter testified that Green (D) indicated to him where the marijuana could be picked up. Porter had previously told the police that Green (D) had actually given him the marijuana. Porter was fully cross-examined at the hearing. At Green's (D) trial, Porter again changed his story alleging that he could not remember who had given him the marijuana since he had been on LSD at the time. The prosecutor then introduced Porter's two earlier statements (i.e., to the police and at the hearing) under the State's (P) prior inconsistent statement exception to the hearsay rule. Green (D) appealed his conviction, alleging that he was denied the opportunity to confront and cross-examine Porter at trial and that the introduction of prior inconsistent statements directly implicating him also violated the Confrontation Clause.

ISSUE: Is the Confrontation Clause satisfied where the defendant has had an opportunity to fully confront and cross-examine a witness at an earlier hearing where a witness can no longer remember the incident or is being impeached through the use of prior inconsistent statements?

HOLDING AND DECISION: Yes. If there was a full opportunity for cross-examination at the earlier hearing, the statements should be admissible at trial. If Porter died, they would be admissible. If he were unavailable at trial they should also be admissible. The Confrontation Clause is satisfied if the witness was available for a thorough cross-examination at an earlier hearing. Moreover, here the witness has repudiated his earlier testimony and is available for cross-examination. His current demeanor is before the jury. The primary objective of the Sixth Amendment is to assure that witnesses will be subject to an oath, cross-examination and observation by a jury. All of these factors were satisfied herein. The hearsay rule exception does not violate the Confrontation Clause since all of the above-mentioned factors are present. While the California rule allows the statements to be introduced to prove the facts asserted, this does not violate the Confrontation Clause. The witness is present, under oath and before the jury. While the statute is constitutional on its face, we must remand to determine if it was constitutionally applied herein and whether the in-custody statements of Porter could be admitted since they were not subject to rights of cross-examination. Remanded.

CONCURRENCE: (J. Harlan) The Confrontation Clause deals with the production of available witnesses, not cross-examination. Cross-examination is not required under the Fourteenth Amendment and would involve a constitutionalization of the hearsay rule removing flexibility from the States. Hearsay rule limits are based on due process concepts not violated by the California rule. I would remand solely to determine the reliability of Porter's custodial statements and the sufficiency of the evidence.

DISSENT: (J. Brennan) When a witness cannot or will not testify concerning earlier testimony, the Confrontation Clause prevents the introduction of such statements.

EDITOR'S ANALYSIS: The Confrontation Clause is not a constitutional shorthand for the hearsay rule. Note that if this were not the case, all hearsay would be excluded since the Clause implies no exceptions. Some hearsay violates due process (e.g., statements by a now absent witness given at a preliminary hearing where the accused was without counsel). Much hearsay, however, clearly does not (e.g., dying declarations, etc.). Note, finally, the practical importance of the California law in Green. If prior inconsistent statements can be used only to impeach a witness, they are not available to a prosecutor (who may not impeach his own witness). By allowing prior inconsistent statements to be offered "for the truth of the matter asserted," however, prosecutors are permitted to reduce the possibility that frightened (by the accused) or genuinely forgetful witnesses may undermine a case at trial.

NOTES:

DUTTON v. EVANS

400 U.S. 74 (1970)

NATURE OF CASE: **Appeal from a murder conviction.**

FACT SUMMARY: **Williams, a co-conspirator with Evans (D), made an admission to a fellow inmate and it was admitted into evidence against Evans (D).**

CONCISE RULE OF LAW: **Statements against penal interest made by a co-conspirator to a third party may be admitted where both the co-conspirator and the third party are available for testimony at trial and the testimony is not devastating to defendant's interests.**

FACTS: Three police officers were murdered. Evans (D) and Williams were separately indicted for murder. Truett, an eyewitness, was granted immunity and testified that Evans (D) was the main participant in the murder. A statement made by Williams to a fellow inmate was also admitted into evidence. The inmate testified that Williams had told him that it was Evans' (D) fault that they were in this situation. The inmate was fully cross-examined and Williams was not called to testify since Evans' (D) counsel felt it would be poor trial tactics. Eighteen other witnesses were called to testify against Evans (D). Evans (D) filed a habeas corpus petition after his conviction. Evans (D) alleged that the hearsay testimony of the inmate violated his Confrontation Clause rights. The State (P) alleged that the testimony was valid under a hearsay exception allowing the statements of one co-conspirator to be admitted into evidence against other conspirators if made during the pendency of the trial and after the conspiracy had been independently proven. The State (P) also alleged that the inmate's testimony was only a minor part of the evidence against Evans (D); was subject to cross-examination; was reliable since it was a statement made by Williams against his own penal interest, and Williams could have been called to testify.

ISSUE: May out-of-court admissions by a co-conspirator, against his penal interests, to a third party be admitted where both the declarant and the co-conspirator are available for cross-examination?

HOLDING AND DECISION: Yes. We decide only the issue herein and decline to make a major ruling on this hearsay rule and the Sixth Amendment. Where there is an indice of truthfulness, both the co-conspirator and the third party are available for cross-examination and the evidence is not devestating to the defendant, we find that the Confrontation Clause has not been violated. Hearsay rules do not individually have to be tested against the Sixth Amendment. There must be a showing of real prejudice. In the case herein, the inmate's testimony played a minor role in the conviction, the statements were made against Williams' penal interests thereby carrying an indicia of truthfulness; both Williams and the inmate were available for cross-examination and the refusal to subpoena Williams by Evans' counsel cannot be held against the State. Affirmed.

CONCURRENCE: (J. Blackmun) The statement was at most harmless error and would not require a reversal.

CONCURRENCE: (J. Harlan) The Confrontation Clause is merely intended to govern the conduct of a trial, i.e., requiring the right to cross-examine witnesses, not to control the rules of evidence. Due process standards give sufficient protection to the rights of the accused.

DISSENT: (J. Marshall) The decision herein is contrary to our holding in Douglas v. Alabama, supra. If the statement could not be admitted in a joint trial of the defendants, it should not be admissible in separate trials. Cross-examination of Williams would not dispel the harm of the inmate's testimony. The indicia of reliability, i.e., statement against penal interest, is the very factor which should have been tested through cross-examination. The statement is so prejudicial that it should not have been allowed without the State first calling Williams.

EDITOR'S ANALYSIS: McCormick points out that if the word "witness" in the Confrontation Clause is read as including hearsay declarants, the literal result would be the exclusion of all hearsay, since the clause contains no exceptions. As indicated by Dutton v. Evans, this has not been the result. Other situations which have been held not to violate the Confrontation Clause are dying declarations, former testimony of now-unavailable witnesses were opportunities for cross-examination was afforded, public records, and entries in the regular course of business.

NOTES:

NELSON, WARDEN v. O'NEIL

SUP. COURT OF THE UNITED STATES, 1971. 402 U.S. 622, 91 S.Ct. 1723, 29 L.Ed. 2d 222

NATURE OF CASE: Criminal action for kidnapping, robbery and vehicle theft.

FACT SUMMARY: O'Neil (D) and Runnels (D) were arrested in a white Cadillac while throwing a gun into an alley.

CONCISE RULE OF LAW: Even though declarant/witness refutes and denies having made an alleged prior statement, cross-examination of such declarant can be full and effective.

FACTS: O'Neil (D) and co-defendant Runnels (D) were identified in a line-up by the owner of a white Cadillac as the men who had kidnapped and robbed him of his money and his car. While in custody, Runnels (D) allegedly made an unsworn statement admitting the crimes and implicating O'Neil as confederate. On the stand in his own defense, Runnels (D) denied having made the statements. The judge instructed the jury to consider the alleged confession only against Runnels (D), not O'Neil (D).

ISSUE: If a declarant denies making an alleged prior statement, can cross-examination be full and effective?

HOLDING AND DECISION: Yes. The majority holds that cross-examination can be "full and effective" even when declarant/witness does not affirm prior statements attributed to him; he need merely have taken the stand and be subject to examination by counsel. The lower court had relied on dicta in earlier cases that confrontation could be effective only when the witness had affirmed the statement as his own. These earlier dicta had probably been based on the theory that cross-examination is effective only when a defendant can challenge a witness, attacking motivation, perception, etc. Under the specific facts of this case, however, O'Neil (D) is better off than if Runnel (D) had in fact affirmed the confession implicating O'Neil (D). Since Runnel's (D) denial in essence supports O'Neil's (D) position, he was denied no rights. Held: Reversed. O'Neil's (D) conviction is reinstated.

DISSENT: (Brennan) The majority is discussing the wrong issue. The question is whether the judge's instruction to the jury was adequate to protect O'Neil (D). The minority says it was not. There is too great a risk that a jury will not follow instructions to disregard the statements of one co-defendant against another. The conviction of O'Neil (D) should be set aside, since the jury obviously considered Runnel's (D) confession in deciding O'Neil's (D) guilt.

EDITOR'S ANALYSIS: The cases, while allowing prior testimony to be introduced if declarant is available as a witness, stop at the point that the declarant refuses to be sworn in or take the stand. In U.S. v. Fiore (2d Cir. 1971), the court held that, since declarant was not "available" for cross-examination to explain/defend his grand jury testimony (since he refused to take the stand), defendant's right of confrontation was denied, and the testimony should not have been introduced.

NOTES:

MANCUSI v. STUBBS

408 U.S. 204 (1972)

NATURE OF CASE: Writ of habeus corpus challenging the validity of a murder conviction.

FACT SUMMARY: Stubbs (D) sought federal habeus corpus, claiming a murder conviction was had in violation of his right to confront witnesses against him, and thus could not be used for assigning second offender status to him in relation to another felony conviction.

CONCISE RULE OF LAW: Convictions based upon retrial are not constitutionally infirm as violative of the right to confront witnesses because testimony from an earlier trial is admitted into evidence, if the witness is found to be unavailable.

FACTS: Stubbs (D) was convicted of a felony in New York and was sentenced as a second offender due to a 1964 Tennessee murder conviction. Stubbs (D) brought a writ of habeus corpus, challenging the validity of the 1964 conviction as violative to the right to confront witnesses against him. Nine years after a 1954 murder conviction, Stubbs (D) sought relief through federal habeus corpus on the grounds of having been denied effective counsel. Relief was granted, and Stubbs (D) was retried in 1964. Holm, a witness at the earlier trial, was subpoenaed, but was living in Sweden and was unavailable and did not appear at the 1964 trial. Satisfied as to Holm's unavailability, the trial court admitted his testimony from the 1954 trial, over Stubbs' (D) objections. Stubbs (D) was again convicted, and the conviction was subsequently affirmed. Stubbs (D) brought this challenge to the 1964 conviction upon conviction in New York to prevent being accorded second offender status for purposes of punishment.

ISSUE: Are convictions based upon retrial constitutionally infirm as violative of the right to confront witnesses where the testimony from the earlier trial is admitted into evidence, if the witness is found to be unavailable.

HOLDING AND DECISION: (Rehnquist, J.) No. Convictions based upon retrial are not constitutionally infirm as violative of the right to confront witnesses where the testimony from the earlier trial is admitted into evidence, where the witness is found to be unavailable. Earlier precedent indicates that a constitutional infirmity might be present where the state does not make a good faith effort to secure the witness's presence at the trial. Such was not the case here. Once is was established that Holm was living in Sweden, there was no power the state could invoke to compel his presence. Given Holm's unavailability, the question becomes the credibility of the testimony offered. Since counsel for Stubbs (D) adequately examined Holm in 1954, the transcript of the first trial bore sufficient indicia of reliability and afforded the trier of fact a satisfactory basis for evaluating the truth of the prior testimony. Thus there was no error in admitting the 1954 testimony, and the 1964 conviction should stand.

EDITOR'S ANALYSIS: A finding of ineffective counsel at a preliminary hearing where the right to counsel attaches does not require a rejection of the testimony; the court will look into the adequacy of the cross-examination. Similarly, restrictions on the right to cross-examine at a preliminary hearing does not render the testimony inherently unreliable.

NOTES:

PARKER v. RANDOLPH

442 U.S. 62 (1979)

NATURE OF CASE: Appeal from conviction for murder.

FACT SUMMARY: Although Randolph (D) confessed to the crime, Randolph (D) claimed it was error to be convicted after confessions made by his co-defendants were also admitted in a joint trial.

CONCISE RULE OF LAW: It is not prejudicial to admit confessions of co-defendants into evidence if the defendant's own confession has been admitted even if co-defendants' confessions are not tested by cross-examination.

FACTS: Randolph (D) and four co-defendants staged an armed robbery to retrieve money lost in poker games with the victim, Douglas, by using a final poker game as a back-drop for the robbery. During the game, Douglas became apprehensive and tried to arm himself but was gunned down in the attempt. Each defendant confessed to the details of the event later. These confessions each corroborated each other and interlocked to form a complete account of the event. Each confession was introduced only against the defendant making the confession. But since all of the defendants were tried in a joint trial and the written confessions were introduced without any defendant testifying, a jury could easily apply different confessions to different defendants without the confessions being tested by cross-examination, Randolph (D) appealed because he was unable to cross-examine the other defendants about their confessions.

ISSUE: Is a defendant prejudicially denied his right to confront witnesses if he is unable to cross-examine co-defendants about their confessions introduced during his trial after he confesses to the same crime?

HOLDING AND DECISION: (J. Rehnquist) No. A distinction can be made between the degree of prejudice involved when a non-testifying co-defendant's confession is used against a defendant claiming to be innocent, and when a non-testifying co-defendant's confession is used against a defendant confessing to the crime. As long as the confession of the co-defendant corroborates, or interlocks with the defendant's confession, the damage of the co-defendant's confession to the defendant's case can be no greater than the damage already done by the defendant's own confession. Here, there was no need for Randolph (D) to have the right to cross-examine the co-defendants in this case, because Randolph (D) could not benefit from it.

CONCURRANCE: (J. Blackmun) The confessions of the co-defendants can be admitted in defendant's trial because they are harmless beyond a reasonable doubt to the defendant's case. The Court should not replace this rule with a per se rule allowing confessions of co-defendants if the defendant has confessed and defendant's confession sufficiently interlocks with co-defendants' confessions.

DISSENT: (J. Stevens) Often, confessions after a crime stem from an untrustworthy passion of guilt or urge to confess. Unreliable confessions by co-defendants may contain much more incriminating evidence than a defendant's confession even if they do interlock to a degree. The stronger incriminations contained in a possibly unreliable co-defendant confession must be tested by cross-examination to uphold the substantive right of the Sixth Amendment's confrontation clause.

EDITOR'S ANALYSIS: The Court was deeply and nearly evenly split on this difficult question. Yet the dissent is not as different from the majority as it may first appear. All probably agree that a defendant is entitled to a constitutional protection only if he can be benefitted by it. The difference stems from whether the justices believe the defendant can be benefitted by cross-examining co-defendants. If a co-defendant's confession is significantly more incriminating to the defendant than the defendant's own confession, the majority would not allow the co-defendant's confession because it was not sufficiently interlocking with the defendant's confession. The dissent would not allow the co-defendant's confession at all.

NOTES:

OHIO v. ROBERTS
448 U.S. 56 (1980)

NATURE OF CASE: **Appeal from reversal of conviction for forgery and possession of stolen credit cards.**

FACT SUMMARY: **The prosecution appealed the reversal of Roberts' (D) conviction of forgery and possession of stolen credit cards, where the court held a preliminary hearing transcript inadmissible.**

CONCISE RULE OF LAW: **Where counsel for defendant avails himself of an adequate opportunity to cross-examine a witness at a preliminary hearing, the transcript of that testimony is sufficiently reliable to be introduced into evidence at a subsequent trial if the witness is unavailable.**

FACTS: Roberts (D) was charged with forgery and possession of stolen credit cards. At his preliminary hearing, counsel for Roberts (D) called as his only defense witness, Anita. Counsel for Roberts (D) attempted to elicit an admission from Anita that she had given Roberts (D) checks and credit cards without informing him that she did not have permission to use them. The questioning took the form of cross-examination and appeared to be in line with the purposes of cross-examination, to challenge the credibility of the witness and the accuracy of the testimony. The attempt was unsuccessful. Roberts (D) was indicted, and new counsel was appointed for him. Anita was subpoenaed five times for four different trial dates, to no avail. At his trial, Roberts (D) took the stand and testified that Anita had given him the checkbook and the credit cards with the understanding he could use them. The prosecution offered the transcript of Anita's testimony for rebuttal, and Roberts (D) objected on confrontation grounds. The trial court conducted a voir dire hearing on the admissibility of the transcript, where Amy the only witness, testified as to the unknown whereabouts of Anita, relating the few, infrequent contacts she had had with Anita in the period of time subsequent to the preliminary hearing. The trial court admitted the transcript, and Roberts (D) was convicted. On appeal, the Court of Appeals reversed, unsatisfied as to the prosecution's good faith effort to secure the absent witness's attendance. The state Supreme Court affirmed this on different grounds, finding that since Anita had not been cross-examined at the preliminary hearing and was absent from the trial, the introduction of the transcript into evidence violated Roberts' (D) right of confrontation.

ISSUE: Where counsel for defendant avails himself of an adequate opportunity to cross-examine a witness at a preliminary hearing, is the transcript of that testimony sufficiently reliable to be introduced into evidence at a subsequent trial if the witness is unavailable?

HOLDING AND DECISION: (Blackmun, J.) Yes. Where counsel for defendant avails himself of an adequate opportunity to cross-examine a witness at a preliminary hearing, the transcript of that testimony is sufficiently reliable to be introduced into evidence at a subsequent trial if the witness is unavailable. Restrictions on the admissibility of hearsay evidence by the right of confrontation takes two forms. First, the prosecution must produce a witness, or demonstrate the witness's unavailability, to use his prior statement. If unavailability of the evidence is established, the reliability of the hearsay statement must be established. Where the statement falls within a firmly rooted hearsay exception, reliability is established; if not, a showing of particularized guarantees of trustworthiness is required. Precedent indicates that where statements are given at a preliminary hearing under circumstances approximating trial conditions, such statements are sufficiently reliable. Factors indicating the existence of trial-like conditions are whether the testimony was given under oath, whether there was an adequate opportunity for cross-examination, and whether counsel for defendant availed himself of the opportunity. In the present case, Anita's testimony was taken under oath. An opportunity to cross-examine was present, and even though the questioning by Roberts' (D) counsel was direct examination, it was in the form of and complied with the purposes of cross-examination. The transcript of the testimony taken under these circumstances is sufficiently reliable to be admitted into evidence if Anita is found to be unavailable. Amy's testimony as to Anita's whereabouts, coupled with the prosecution's unsuccessful attempts to subpoena her, support the conclusion that Anita was constitutionally unavailable for Roberts' (D) trial. Judgment of the State Supreme Court reversed.

DISSENT: (Brennan, J.) The improbability of successfully securing Anita's presence at the trial, does not relieve the prosecution of its burden to make a good faith effort to secure her presence. The perfunctory steps that the prosecution took in this case do not suffice to support a finding of unavailability.

EDITOR'S ANALYSIS: The argument that at preliminary hearings, strategy often dictates that no cross-examination take place because of the opportunity to cross-examine at trial is not looked on favorably by the courts, which treat the situation as similar to where depositions are entered into evidence. The court in that situation attaches no significance to the extent of cross-examination, once the deponent becomes available.

NOTES:

DAVIS v. ALASKA

415 U.S. 308 (1974)

NATURE OF CASE: **Appeal from a robbery conviction.**

FACT SUMMARY: **The court refused to allow Davis (D) to impeach a witness on the basis of his adjudication as a juvenile delinquent.**

CONCISE RULE OF LAW: **A state's policy of protecting juvenile offenders must give way to an accused's right to effective cross-examination where bias can be established.**

FACTS: A safe was stolen from a bar and was found abandoned near Green's parents' farm. Green, a juvenile offender on probation for theft, informed the police that he had seen two men in a Chevrolet parked on the road near where the safe had been found. Davis (D) and another man were subsequently apprehended. Traces of paint which could have come from the safe were found in their car's trunk. Green testified to his identification of Davis (D). Because of Alaska's (P) policy of protecting juvenile offenders, Davis' (D) attorney was not permitted to bring out Green's record or probationary status. Davis (D) was foreclosed from establishing through such disclosures a bias and an alternative reason for the identification. Davis (D) argued that he had been denied the right to effectively cross-examine Green and that his Confrontation Clause rights were superior to the interest of the State (P) in protecting juveniles.

ISSUE: May a state's policy of protecting juvenile offenders interfere with an accused's right to effective cross-examination?

HOLDING AND DECISION: No. Where meaningful avenues of cross-examination are foreclosed by a state's policy of protecting juveniles, the Confrontation Clause has been violated. The case herein does not merely involve casting doubt on the general veracity of a witness. Here, a positive bias may be established casting grave doubt on the identification. Green was on probation for robbery. The safe was found near his parents' farm. Green was certainly a possible suspect and placing the blame on others and/or the need to make a positive identification were considerations of which the jury should have been informed. Foreclosure of this avenue of questioning was a denial of effective cross-examination. Reversed.

DISSENT: (White, J.) There is no constitutional principle at stake. Limiting cross-examination is within the discretion of the trial court, and on review, the state appeals court found no substantial harm to the defense. Second-guessing them is improper, since this court is no better able to make these determinations than they were.

CONCURRENCE: (Stewart, J.) The Court's holding today does not confer a right in every case to impeach the general credibility of a witness through cross-examination about past delinquency adjudications or criminal convictions. Only where the circumstances of the case dictate necessity will such a right be conferred.

EDITOR'S ANALYSIS: Inquiry for impeachment is usually confined to the prominent motives for untruthful testimony: interest in the suit which necessarily tends to bias, and other circumstances showing bias which are not too remote. If impeachment evidence is too prejudicial and is irrelevant to the witness' propensity for truth, its admission may be deemed reversible error. Grudt v. City of Los Angeles, 2 Cal. 3d 575 (1970).

NOTES:

CHAMBERS v. MISSISSIPPI

SUP.CT.OF U.S.,1973. 410 U.S.284, 93 S.Ct.1038

NATURE OF CASE: **Appeal from conviction for murder.**

FACT SUMMARY: **Chambers (D) was convicted of murder after not being allowed to show that a witness whom he called to testify confessed to the killing to three of his friends on the ground that such confessions were hearsay.**

CONCISE RULE OF LAW: **Where constitutional rights directly affecting the ascertainment of guilt are implicated, the hearsay rule may not be applied mechanically so to defeat the ends of justice.**

FACTS: Chambers (D) was tried and convicted of murdering a policeman during a confrontation between a few policemen and several townspeople when the former were attempting to arrest one of the latter. McDonald, a town resident, after talking to Rev. Stokes, agreed to see Chambers' (D) lawyers and confess to the killing. He did so, was jailed, but was later released upon repudiating his confession, which he claimed was prompted by a promise of a share in a tort recovery which Chambers (P) would get from the town. At trial, Chambers (D) tried to show that McDonald committed the crime. Hardin testified that he saw McDonald, his long-time friend, shoot the officer. Additionally, Chambers (D) sought to show that McDonald not only confessed to his lawyers, but that he confessed to three of his friends. Chambers (D) called McDonald to testify when the state (P) failed to do so. McDonald again repudiated his confession. The court denied Chambers' (D) motion that McDonald be declared an adverse witness. It also prevented three of McDonald's friends from testifying that he confessed to them on the ground that such a confession was hearsay. Under Missippi (P) law, a person who presents a witness vouches for his credibility, and the hearsay exception for declarations against interest applies only when that interest is pecuniary, while here it was not. Chambers (D) appealed his conviction on due process grounds.

ISSUE: Where constitutional rights directly affecting the ascertainment of guilt are implicated, may the hearsay rule be applied mechanically so to defeat the ends of justice?

HOLDING AND DECISION: (J. Powell) No. Where constitutional rights directly affecting the ascertainment of guilt are implicated, the hearsay rule may not be applied mechanically to defeat the ends of justice. Chambers (D) was not allowed to subject McDonald's repudiation and alibi to cross-examination. Cross-examination is fundamental to assuring the accuracy of the truth-determining process. The voucher rule, which does not allow a party to impeach his own witness, bears little usefulness to the criminal process. Here, it not only precluded cross-examination, it restricted the scope of direct examination. The right to confront and cross-examine has never depended on who put the witness on the stand. As for declarations against interest, most states will not admit them even when they are against a penal interest. But here, several circumstances assured the declaration's reliability. (1) Each of McDonald's confessions was spontaneous and made shortly after the killing; (2) each one was corroborated by some other evidence; (3) each was unquestionably against interest; and (4) McDonald was present in the courtroom to explain under oath his declaration. The testimony was absolutely critical to Chamber's (D) defense. Reversed and remanded.

EDITOR'S ANALYSIS: The court specifically noted that by this case it was not creating any new principles in constitutional law. Rather, the trial rules in question were not "in accord with traditional and fundamental standards of due process." Further, the decision was not intended to diminish each state's ability to create its own trial rules. It would appear arguable, however, that the court believes hearsay statements should be admitted when trustworthy. The court does not require the state's to go that far as long as their rules do not offend notions of due process.

NOTES:

GREEN v. GEORGIA

Sup. Ct. of U.S., 442 U.S. 95, Sup. Ct. 2150 (1979)

NATURE OF CASE: **Appeal from a murder conviction.**

FACT SUMMARY: **The trial court refused to admit Pasby's testimony that Moore had said to him he had committed the murder and sent Green (D) away on an errand, holding it was inadmissible hearsay.**

CONSCISE RULE OF LAW: **The hearsay rule will not apply where exclusion of the evidence would deny a criminal defendant due process of law.**

FACTS: Green (D) and Moore were indicted together for the rape and murder, yet were tried seperately. At Moore's trial, the State (P) introduced testimony of Pasby who said Moore had confided in him that he killed the victim after ordering Green (D) to run an errand. The statement had been made spontaneously and Pasby was a close friend of Moore's. After Moore's conviction, Green (D) was tried, and was prohibited from introducing Pasby's testimony by the trial court which held it was inadmissible hearsay. Green (D) was convicted of murder and received a capital sentence. He appealed, yet the Supreme Court of Georgia upheld the conviction and sentence. Green (D) appealed to the U.S. Supreme Court.

ISSUE: Will the hearsay rule apply even where exclusion of the evidence would constitute a denial of due process to a criminal defendant?

HOLDING AND DECISION: (Per Curriam) No. The hearsay rule will not apply where exclusion of the evidence would constitute a denial of due process to the criminal defendant. In this case the testimony was highly relevant to a critical issue in the case. Its spontaneous nature and the fact it was spoken to a close friend support its reliability. Further, the statements were against Moore's interest indicating he had nothing to gain by lying in this way. Finally, the State (P) considered the testimony sufficiently reliable to use it to convict Moore of a capital crime. As a result, under these circumstances, it would defeat the ends of justice and deny Green (D) due process of law to apply the hearsay rule to exclude the testimony. Reversed.

DISSENT: (J. Rehnquist) The Court's ruling is without constitutional justification. It is a maxime of evidence law that certain items are admissible against one party yet not another.

EDITOR'S ANALYSIS: This case applies the rule articulated in Chambers v. Mississippi, 410 U.S. 284 (9173). In that case the court held that the hearsay could not be invoked to exclude evidence in a criminal trial if the result of the exclusion would be the denial of a fair trial. This exception therefore constitutionally based and applies only in criminal trials. Its application is rare and generally a criminal defendant is limited in his use of hearsay to specific exceptions.

NOTES:

IN THE MATTER OF MYRON FARBER

78 N.J. 259, 394 A.2d 330 (1978); cert. denied 439 U.S. 997, 99 S.Ct. 598, 58 L.Ed.2d 670

NATURE OF CASE: Appeal from contempt citations.

FACT SUMMARY: Farber (D), a reporter for the New York Times, was cited for contempt after refusing to disclose certain investigative documents.

CONCISE RULE OF LAW: Newspeople are not constitutionally privileged to withhold duly subpoenaed documents.

FACTS: The New York Times Company and Myron Farber, a reporter employed by the newspaper, challenged judgments of civil and criminal contempt entered against them. The proceedings were instituted in an ongoing murder trial of Dr. Mario E. Jascalevich, as a result of their failure to comply with two subpoenas duces tecum, directing them to produce certain documents and materials compiled by one or both of them in the course of Farber's (D) investigative reporting of certain allegedly criminal activities. Farber (D) claimed a First Amendment privilege to refrain from revealing information sought by the subpoenas duces tecum for the reason that, if the material were divulged, confidential sources of such information would be made public.

ISSUE: Are newspeople constitutionally privileged to withhold duly subpoenaed documents?

HOLDING AND DECISION: (J. Mountain) No. The Supreme Court, in Branzburg v. Hayes, 408 U.S. 665 (1972), held that the First Amendment affords no privilege to a newsman to refuse to appear before a grand jury and testify as to relevant information he possesses, even though in so doing he may divulge confidential sources. Thus, there is no authority for the proposition that newsmen are constitutionally privileged to withhold duly subpoenaed documents material to the prosecution or defense of a criminal case. Further, the Sixth Amendment and the New Jersey State Constitution afford a defendant in a criminal prosecution the right to compel the attendance of witnesses and the production of documents and other material for which he may have, or may believe he has, a legitimate need in preparing or undertaking his defense. It also means that witnesses properly summoned will be required to testify, and that material demanded by a properly phrased subpoena duces tecum will be forthcoming and available for appropriate examination and use. These constitutional provisions override any state laws designed to protect the confidentiality of a reporter's sources of information. Affirmed.

DISSENT: (J. Pashman) Prior cases have held that the First Amendment will not always prevent forced disclosure of a reporter's confidential sources and information, but implied state legislatures were not powerless to alter that result. In passing its shield law, New Jersey's legislature did an overall weighing and balancing between freedom of the press and other assertedly compelling interests, thereby deciding that there should not be a case-by-case weighing. It passed the law to ensure that in every case the right to nondisclosure would be paramount. This is a permissible exercise of legislative authority which, as the product of a co-equal branch of government, must be respected by the courts.

EDITOR'S ANALYSIS: In this case, Farber (D) and the New York Times argued that the New Jersey "shield" law protected against the disclosure of confidential sources of information. That statute read in part ". . . a person engaged in the gathering or procuring . . . of news for the general public . . . has a privilege to refuse to disclose, in any legal or quasi-legal proceeding . . . the source, author, means, agency or person from or through whom any information was procured. . . ."N.J.S.A. 2A: 84A-21 and 21a.

NOTES:

PRICHARD v. UNITED STATES

181 F.2d 326 (6th Cir. 1950), aff'd 339 U.S. 974 (1950)

NATURE OF CASE: Appeal from conviction for conspiracy to stuff ballot boxes.

FACT SUMMARY: Prichard (D), who was convicted of conspiracy in connection with ballot box stuffing, appealed on the basis that testimony relating to a conversation between Prichard (D) and Judge Avery, a close personal friend and active judge in the district where Prichard (D) practiced, should have been protected from disclosure by the attorney-client privilege.

CONCISE RULE OF LAW: Conversations between a judge and another person which concern matters which fall within the scope of the judge's official duties and responsibilities are not afforded protection under the attorney-client privilege.

FACTS: Prichard (D), a distinguished attorney, became involved in election fraud activities. After consulting with his attorney, Prichard (D) sought the advice of Judge Avery, a long-time personal friend and an active member of the judiciary. Earlier that same day, Judge Avery had called a grand jury to investigate election frauds in the county and was to instruct the grand jury as to its duties and the scope of its investigation. The district judge hearing the case admitted testimony concerning the conversation over Prichard's (D) claim of privilege. Prichard (D) was convicted of conspiracy and appealed.

ISSUE: Are conversations between a judge and another person which concern matters that fall within the scope of the judge's official duties and responsibilities afforded protection against disclosure by the attorney-client privilege?

HOLDING AND DECISION: (Simons, J.) No. While not deciding whether superior court judges could never enter into an attorney-client relationship, here the conversation was not protected from disclosure by the attorney-client privilege. Keeping in mind the following: the importance of the particular position held by Judge Avery; the scope of his official duties, which included the impanelling and instructing of a grand jury investigating election fraud; and the general notion of judicial propriety and the American Bar Association Canons of Judicial Conduct, it would be impossible for Judge Avery to have entered into an attorney-client relationship with Prichard (D), whose conduct would have come under investigation by the grand jury under the Judge's charge. Knowledge that came to Judge Avery while carrying out his duties with respect to the grand jury could not be reserved by him in confidence. The advice sought by Prichard (D) was more like a valued friend's advice rather than the legal advice of the type normally protected by the attorney-client privilege. Finally, Prichard's (D) knowledge of the judge's functions were found to rob his request for protection under the privilege of an element of good faith. A conversation between a judge and a person so situated would not be afforded protection under the attorney-client privilege, and the district court judge did not err in admitting the testimony. Affirmed.

EDITOR'S ANALYSIS: According to McCormick on Evidence, 3rd ed., there seems to be no justification for a privilege between an individual and a judge if the policy motive behind the privilege is the furtherance of the administration of justice by encouraging full client disclosure, since the performance of a judge's duties does not require this type of disclosure. See Lindsay v. People, 66 Colo. 343, 181 P. 531 (1919), for a discussion of whether a judge in juvenile court stands in a position with regard to confidential disclosures made to him by children who come before him.

NOTES:

UNITED STATES v. PAPE

144 F.2d 778 (2d Cir. 1944)

NATURE OF CASE: Appeal from conviction for transporting a woman in interstate commerce "for the purpose of prostitution, debauchery and other immoral purposes."

FACT SUMMARY: The attorney for Pape (D) was required to testify that Pape (D) had retained him and paid him to obtain the release of a prostitute at an earlier appearance, and Pape (D) appealed.

CONCISE RULE OF LAW: Conversations between an attorney and his client with respect to the fact of retainer or the identity of a client are not protected from disclosure by the attorney-client privilege.

FACTS: The attorney, Buckley, was retained by Pape (D) to represent both Pape (D) and a woman, both of whom were implicated in an indictment for transporting a woman in interstate commerce for the purpose of prostitution, debauchery, and other immoral purposes. Buckley first appeared for the woman and obtained her release in his custody. At Pape's (D) trial, Buckley was required to testify that Pape (D) had retained him and had paid him to obtain the release of the woman. Pape (D) was convicted and appealed.

ISSUE: Are communications between an attorney and his client as to the fact of retainer or the identity of a client protected from disclosure by the attorney-client privilege?

HOLDING AND DECISION: (Clark, J.) No. The attorney-client privilege extends only to confidential communications, and communications as to the fact of retainer or the identity of a client are not confidential to bring them within the protection of the privilege. No importance attached to the fact that Buckley was representing both Pape (D) and the woman. The policy behind the privilege, to promote freedom of consultation, does not apply to communications regarding retainers or the identity of clients. The general rule, that relevant evidence is freely admissible unless privileged, applied in this case. Finding no privilege, the communications between Pape (D) and his attorney were not protected from disclosure by the attorney-client privilege, and that testimony as to such matters was properly received by the trial court. Affirmed.

DISSENT: (Hand, J.) The timing of Pape (D) with respect to when he retained counsel for himself and when he retained counsel for the woman is of importance. If Pape (D) had retained Buckley to first represent himself, the subsequent retention of Buckley to represent the woman could be considered a communication between an attorney and his client with regard to Pape's (D) defense. In such a case, it would be conceivable that a communication of this type should be afforded protection against disclosure by the attorney-client privilege.

EDITOR'S ANALYSIS: The dissent comes closer to the real issue than the majority, in recognizing that there could be instances where the fact of a retainer or the identity of a client could be incriminating. The real issue should not focus on the severity of harm that might be occasioned on the defendant, but rather on whether the protection afforded aids the attorney in performing a legitimate function within his professional role.

NOTES:

COUCH v. UNITED STATES

SUPREME CT. OF U.S., 1973. U.S. 93 S. Ct. 611

NATURE OF CASE: Action to enforce Internal Revenue summons.

FACT SUMMARY: Couch's (D) accountant was served with a summons ordering him to produce tax records of Couch (D) that were in his possession.

CONCISE RULE OF LAW: When a party has substantially divested himself of possession of a private writing, he is disqualified from asserting that the writing will incriminate him in violation of the Fifth Amendment.

NOTES:

FACTS: For several years, Couch (D) had turned over her tax records to an independent accountant. When it was learned that there was a possibility of a tax fraud, the IRS issued a summons to the accountant ordering him to produce the records. When Couch (D) learned of this, she had the accountant give the records to her attorney, and refused to produce them.

ISSUE: May a taxpayer invoke the privilege against self-incrimination to prevent the production of her business and tax records in the possession of her accountant?

HOLDING AND DECISION: No. Where a party has substantially divested himself of possession of a private writing, he is disqualified from asserting that the writing will incriminate him in violation of the Fifth Amendment. The Fifth Amendment privilege is a personal one. It attaches to the person, not to the information that may incriminate him. The privilege prevents the person from being a witness against himself, it does not prevent incriminating evidence from other sources. Here, there was more than a slight divestment of possession of the tax records, the accountant had them in his possession for several years. When the divestment of possession is so great, the owner of the writing can no longer assert that its production would violate her Fifth Amendment rights. There is also no accountant-client privilege recognized in federal law, therefore, the summons must be obeyed.

EDITOR'S ANALYSIS: The privilege, as stated, is personal and, therefore, does not attach to writings. However, to be admissible, a writing must be authenticated by its custodian, or the person in possession of the writing. If the owner of the document is the same person who has possession, the privilege against self-incrimination will prevent the admission of the document into evidence. This is not because the privilege attaches to the document, but because the required authentication would incriminate the owner. Therefore, in this case, as the accountant was the custodian of the records, he would not be incriminated by authenticating the documents.

UNITED STATES v. SCHMIDT

343 F. Supp. 444 (M.D. Pa. 1972)

NATURE OF CASE: Action seeking enforcement of a summons.

FACT SUMMARY: The IRS (P) brought this action seeking compliance with a summons issued to Schmidt (D), an accountant, who refused, claiming attorney-client privilege.

CONCISE RULE OF LAW: Not included in casebook excerpt.

FACTS: The McCues retained a lawfirm (SWP). SWP in turn employed Schmidt (D), an accountant. An agreement entered into by Schmidt (D) and SWP made clear that all of Schmidt's (D) services were to be performed at the written request of SWP, that the McCues were clients of SWP, and that Schmidt's (D) services were required by SWP to give accurate and complete legal advice and consultation. All of Schmidt's (D) work product was made the exclusive property of SWP, and information obtained by Schmidt (D) was to be considered confidential. The IRS issued a summons requiring Schmidt (D) to appear and testify as to the tax liability of the McCues, and Schmidt (D) refused to answer questions, asserting the attorney-client privilege. The IRS then sought judicial enforcement to summons.

ISSUE: Can the circumstances of an accountant's employment relationship with a law firm be such as to allow the accountant to assert the attorney-client privilege?

HOLDING AND DECISION: (Sheridan, C.J.) Not included in casebook excerpt.

EDITOR'S ANALYSIS: The case is merely here to present the question raised in the issue to the reader. The cases on the subject are not consistent. There is authority for holding both ways for the ability of an accountant to assert the attorney-client privilege when employed by the attorney. The court in this case found vital in its determination the question of whether or not the information sought contained confidential material transmitted for purposes of obtaining legal advice.

NOTES:

FISHER v. UNITED STATES

Sup.Ct.of U.S.,1976. 425 U.S.391, 96 S.Ct.1569, 48 L.Ed.2d 39

NATURE OF CASE: **Appeal of an order regarding a summons directing the production of documents.**

FACT SUMMARY: **After a visit by an IRS agent, a taxpayer obtained the documents his accountant used in preparing his tax returns and then turned them over to his lawyer, Fisher (D).**

CONCISE RULE OF LAW: **The Fifth Amendment privilege against self-incrimination does not protect against the proper acquisition or use of private information which does not involve compelled testimonial self-incrimination of some sort.**

FACTS: A taxpayer was visited by an IRS agent in connection with an investigation of possible civil or criminal liability under the federal income tax laws. He immediately obtained from his accountant certain documents relating to the preparation by the accountant of his tax returns and handed them over to his lawyer, Fisher (D). Fisher (D) was retained to help the taxpayer in connection with the investigation. The IRS served a summons, directing Fisher (D) to produce the documents. Despite protestations that such would violate the client's privilege against self-incrimination, the court ordered the summons enforced. An appeal was taken, and the order was upheld. Fisher's (D) subsequent appeal was combined with an appeal in a similar case.

ISSUE: Does the Fifth Amendment privilege protect against the proper acquisition of private information which does not involve compelled testimonial self-incrimination?

HOLDING AND DECISION: No. The privilege against self-incrimination within the Fifth Amendment does not protect against the proper acquisition or use of private information which does not involve compelled testimonial self-incrimination of some sort. Here, the taxpayer is not being compelled to do anything and the papers involved do not rise to the level of testimonial communication. He retains any privilege he ever had not to be compelled to testify against himself and not to be compelled to himself produce papers in his posssession. As to the attorney-client privilege, it applies to and protects documents in the hands of an attorney only if they would have been privileged in the hands of the client by reason of the Fifth Amendment. In this case, the documents sought do not involve compelled testimonial self-incrimination. Thus, the Fifth Amendment privilege would not apply were they in the hands of the taxpayer. That means, the attorney-client privilege does not cover them in the hands of Fisher (D). Affirmed.

EDITOR'S ANALYSIS: The courts have determined that the Fifth Amendment privilege is not applicable to many types of compelled production because what is produced does not rise to the level of testimonial communication. Thus, an accused can be required to submit a handwriting exemplar, submit a voice exemplar, or even put on an article of clothing worn by the perpetrator of the crime.

NOTES:

CLARK v. STATE

CT.OF CRIM.APP., TEX., 1953. 159 Tex.Cr.R.187, 261 S.W.2d 339

NATURE OF CASE: Appeal from a conviction for murder.

FACT SUMMARY: Bartz, a telephone operator, eavesdropped during a telephone conversation between Clark (D) and his attorney in which he (D) admitted to the murder of his wife and was advised to dispose of the murder weapon. At trial, Bartz' testimony was admitted despite the objection that it was precluded by application of the attorney-client privilege.

CONCISE RULE OF LAW: The attorney-client privilege may not be invoked as a bar to the testimony of an eavesdropper, and does not apply to communications which are in furtherance of criminal activity.

FACTS: On the evening that she had obtained a divorce from her husband, Clark's (D) wife was found murdered. The findings of a firearms expert indicated she had been killed by the same type of gun as was owned by Clark (D). Other evidence at trial included the testimony of Marjorie Bartz, a telephone operator who testified that she had placed a call from Clark (D) to his attorney on the evening of Mrs. Clark's murder. Bartz admitted that she eavesdropped during the conversation, and heard Clark (D) admit to the murder of his wife. She testified that he (D) was then advised by his attorney to "get rid of the weapon." Clark (D) was convicted of murder, but argued on appeal that Bartz' testimony should have been excluded since it related to a privileged communication between a lawyer and his client.

ISSUE: May an eavesdropper testify to the contents of an ostensibly confidential communication between an attorney and his client?

HOLDING AND DECISION: Yes. Evidence, even if obtained by eavesdropping, is admissible provided that it is relevant. And, since the eavesdropper occupies no confidential relationship to either party, such evidence may not be excluded by invocation of the attorney-client privilege, notwithstanding that the testimony relates to a conversation which both the client and his attorney believed was confidential. Therefore, Bartz' testimony was properly admitted, and Clark's (D) conviction must be affirmed.

ON MOTION FOR REHEARING: The attorney-client privilege is justified by the public's interest in encouraging disclosure to an attorney of all facts material to a client's case. But this laudable interest may not be abused by parties who would invoke the privilege to protect against communications in which a client is advised of ways in which to avoid apprehension for a crime. When an attorney advises his client of how best to avoid prosecution, he becomes an accessory to his client's crime. Since such conduct is not within the realm of legitimate professional employment, communications of this type are not entitled to the protection afforded by the attorney-client privilege.

EDITOR'S ANALYSIS: Courts permitting an eavesdropper to disclose the contents of a conversation between an attorney and his client generally justify their narrow application of the privilege by pointing out that rules of evidence which tend to frustrate truth ascertainment are entitled to strict construction. The Clark court's holding that the privilege may not be asserted to protect against disclosure of communications in furtherance of a crime is in accord with the weight of authority.

NOTES:

STATE v. OLWELL

64 Wash. 2d. 828, 394 P.2d. 681 (1964)

NATURE OF CASE: Appeal from order finding attorney in contempt of court.

FACT SUMMARY: Olwell (D) appealed from an order finding him in contempt of court for failure to answer questions concerning his failure to produce material evidence of a crime pursuant to a subpoena issued in connection with a coroner's inquest.

CONCISE RULE OF LAW: Material evidence of a crime obtained through confidential communications with a client is protected for a reasonable time from compulsory disclosure by the attorney-client privilege, if it is of some value in the preparation of the defense of the client's case.

FACTS: Gray and Warren engaged in a fight in which Warren was mortally wounded by knife wounds. Gray was arrested the following day, admitted to the stabbing, and proceeded to cooperate with the authorities in the investigation of the homicide. Two days later, Olwell (D) was retained as Gray's counsel. Before the coroner's inquest, Olwell (D) was served with a subpoena requiring him to bring "all knives relating to Gray, . . . " to the inquest. At some time prior to the inquest, Olwell (D) came into possession of a knife that at the time was considered a possible murder weapon. It was not clear whether Olwell (D) obtained he knife through his own investigation or as a result of a communication made by Gray to Olwell (D) pursuant to their attorney-client relationship. At the inquest, Olwell (D) refused to answer questions concerning the knife and did not produce the knife, claiming the information was protected by the attorney-client privilege. Olwell (D) was adjudged to be in contempt of court, and from this judgment he appealed.

ISSUE: Is material evidence of a crime obtained through confidential communications with a client protected for a reasonable time from compulsory disclosure by the attorney-client privilege, if it is of some value in the preparation of the defense of the client's case?

HOLDING AND DECISION: (Donworth, J.) Yes. Material evidence of a crime obtained through confidential communications with a client is protected for a reasonable time by the attorney-client privilege, against compulsory disclosure, if it is of some value in the preparation of the defense of the client's case. To be protected by the attorney-client privilege, information or objects obtained by an attorney must be communicated or delivered to the attorney by the client. Communications concerning an alleged crime are protected by the attorney-client privilege as long as the attorney-client relationship is established. The court must balance the value of asserting the privilege against the public's interest in the criminal investigation process. Such a balancing process leads to the conclusion that an attorney could refuse to produce material evidence of a crime for a reasonable period of time. After a reasonable period of time, the attorney as an officer of the court, should of his own motion turn the evidence over to the prosecution. The prosecution is then required to take great care in guarding the interests protected by the privilege. Thus a balance is struck between the competing interests. Here, the court assumed that the knife was obtained as a result of a confidential communication. The subpoena issued was invalid on its face because it required Olwell (D) to give information received confidentially from Gray. That would be equivalent to requiring Gray to testify against himself. Olwell's (D) refusal to testify should not be found contemptuous. (The court determined that Olwell (D) could not assert Gray's privilege against self-incrimination, finding no reason to extend the privilege to information already protected by the attorney-client privilege.) Order reversed with instructions to dismiss.

EDITOR'S ANALYSIS: As noted, the burden is on the prosecution to prevent prejudicial disclosure of the source of such evidence. The privilege will be defeated if abused, for example if the privilege is asserted to hide evidence of a crime or to hinder the prosecution in the preparation of its case.

NOTES:

IN RE RYDER

263 F.Supp.360 (1967)

NATURE OF CASE: **Appeal from a suspension.**

FACT SUMMARY: **While Ryder (D) was defending a robbery suspect, he transferred money and a weapon from the client's safety deposit box to his own.**

CONCISE RULE OF LAW: **The attorney-client privilege does not protect an attorney who attempts to hide the fruits and instrumentalities of a crime.**

FACTS: Ryder (D) was defending Cook on a robbery charge. After Cook had retained Ryder (D) as his attorney, Ryder (D) transferred a weapon and money from Cook's safety deposit box to his own at Cook's request. Cook informed him that a man had paid him $500 to place the money and weapon in the box. Ryder (D) did not believe the story. Ryder (D) asked a number of lawyers, professors and an ex-judge about the propriety of his actions. Cook was subsequently arrested and a warrant to search both Ryder's (D) and Cook's safety deposit boxes turned up the weapon and the money. Ryder (D) was deemed guilty of unprofessional conduct and his privilege to practice law in federal court was suspended.

ISSUE: May an attorney violate the law on behalf of his client's interest under the guise of the attorney-client privilege?

HOLDING AND DECISION: No. It is an abuse of the attorney's professional responsibility to knowingly secrete either the fruits or instrumentalities of a crime. While Ryder (D) urged Cook to reveal the evidence to the police, he could not participate in hiding the evidence under the guise of the attorney-client privilege. The privilege merely allows the attorney to remain silent, not to actively participate in illegal activity. Ryder (D), by hiding the weapon and money, became an accessory after the fact. This is far beyond the scope of the privilege. The suspension is affirmed.

EDITOR'S ANALYSIS: The death of the client does not destroy the attorney-client privilege. However, there are circumstances in which the privilege will not prevent disclosure by the attorney. Hence, where a disclosure would be for the benefit of a decedent's estate, the attorney may be compelled to testify as to confidential communications. Sometimes the testator will be found to have waived the privilege in his lifetime, as by directing the attorney to act as an attesting witness. Wigmore argued, as to will contests, that communications of the client to his lawyer as to the making of a will are intended to be confidential during the client's lifetime, but that this is a temporary confidentiality not intended to require secrecy after the client's death.

NOTES:

HICKMAN v. TAYLOR

329 U.S. 495 (1947)

NATURE OF CASE: Appeal from a judgment of civil contempt for failure to produce work product pursuant to discovery request.

FACT SUMMARY: In connection with a suit in federal court under the Jones Act, the attorney for Taylor (D) was held in contempt for failure to produce documents, reports, memoranda and other materials gathered in preparation for litigation and sought by opposing counsel through the use of interrogatories.

CONCISE RULE OF LAW: The Federal Rules of Civil Procedure relating to the use of discovery devices do not require the production as of right of the oral and written statements of witnesses or other information obtained by an adverse party's counsel in preparation for possible litigation after a claim has arisen.

FACTS: A tugboat sank while engaged in towing operations, drowning five crewmen. The cause of the accident was unknown. Taylor (D) obtained counsel to defend against potential suits by representatives of the deceased crew members. Fortenbaugh, the counsel retained, took written statements from the survivors of the accident and interviewed other persons connected with the accident in some way, in some cases making memoranda of what was said. Claims from the representatives of all five deceased crew members were eventually brought, four of which were settled out of court. The fifth brought suit in federal court under the Jones Act, and sought to discover the written statements and other information that Fortenbaugh had obtained in preparation for the litigation. Taylor (D) and his counsel refused to produce the material, claiming the material was privileged. The District Court found no applicable privilege and ordered counsel for Taylor (D) to produce the requested material. Taylor (D) and Fortenbaugh refused and were adjudged in contempt. They appealed, and the judgment of contempt was reversed by the Court of Appeals. Hickman (P) then petitioned the Supreme Court for review.

ISSUE: Do the Federal Rules of Civil Procedure relating to the use of discovery devices require the production as of right of the oral and written statements, or other information obtained by an adverse party's counsel in preparation for possible litigation, after a claim has arisen?

HOLDING AND DECISION: (Murphy, J.) No. Pre-trial discovery mechanisms under the Federal Rules should be accorded broad and liberal treatment, while the material sought in this case was outside the attorney-client privilege, this was not the key to answering the issue at hand. The position of an attorney in our system of justice required that he be able to work with a certain degree of privacy, free from intrusion from opposing counsel. To make the work product of an attorney available to opposing counsel on demand would not serve the interests of either the clients involved or the interests of justice. Written materials obtained in preparation of litigation would not be free from discovery in all cases, but absent any showing of necessity, or demonstration that the denial of discovery would result in hardship or injustice, the Federal Rules of Civil Procedure do not require the production as of right of the oral and written statements of witnesses, or other information obtained by an adverse party's counsel in preparation for possible litigation, once a claim has arisen. Affirmed.

EDITOR'S ANALYSIS: Hickman v. Taylor is the landmark case with respect to the attorney work product privilege and attempts to strike a balance between the desire to have full and open discovery with the need of the attorney to be able to prepare his case and legal strategy without needless and undue interference. Questions still remain with respect to peripheral issues, such as when work is done not in preparation for litigation or is done in preparation for other litigation, or material is prepared by someone not under the direction of the attorney, but with an eye towards possible litigation.

NOTES:

RADIANT BURNERS v. AMERICAN GAS ASSOCIATION

207 F. Supp. 771 (N.D. Ill. 1962), rev'd, 320 F.2d 314 (7th Cir. 1963)

NATURE OF CASE: Proceeding involving corporate claim of attorney-client privilege.

FACT SUMMARY: Counsel for American Gas Association (D), in compliance with discovery and pre-trial procedures set forth by the Judicial Council for protracted anti-trust litigation, presented files of documents to the court for a determination of whether they were protected by the attorney-client privilege.

CONCISE RULE OF LAW: A corporation is not entitled to make a claim under the attorney-client privilege.

FACTS: Pursuant to the procedures established by the Judicial Council for protracted anti-trust litigation, counsel for AGA (D) provided files of documents to the court for a determination of whether they should be considered privileged under the attorney-client privilege, and thus not be disclosed to Radiant Burners' (P) counsel or not privileged and delivered to Radiant Burners' (P) counsel for inspection. All documents save a very few were disposed of, and upon further consideration of these few documents, the court entertained the question of whether the attorney-client privilege should be available to corporations at all.

ISSUE: Is a corporation entitled to make a claim of the attorney-client privilege in order to prevent disclosure of certain documents to opposing counsel?

HOLDING AND DECISION: (Campbell, C. J.) No. The privilege, like the privilege against self-incrimination, is personal in nature and has its genesis in common law. A corporation is a creature of the state, and thus the privilege cannot be extended to a corporation absent legislation so providing. The confidential nature of the communications traditionally protected under the privilege creates problems in extending the privilege to corporate clients. To do so would require a substantial expansion of the notions of what constitutes a "client" and what constitutes a "confidential communication" within the meaning of privilege. While other privileges, such as the attorney work product privilege, would still be available to corporations, because of the personal nature of the privilege at common law and because of the confidentiality problems created by the privilege's application to corporate clients, corporations cannot be entitled to make a claim under the attorney-client privilege.

EDITOR'S ANALYSIS: The availability of the attorney-client privilege to a corporate client had never been questioned until the present case. A rush of comment followed the decision, almost entirely negative. The Seventh Circuit Court of Appeals, in reversing Campbell, found that the attorney-client privilege was enacted to facilitate the working of justice, without reference to the corporate or non-corporate nature of the client. Questions concerning the privilege in this context now revolve around what members of the corporation should be allowed to invoke the privilege, and what communications will be considered privileged.

NOTES:

UPJOHN CO. v. UNITED STATES

U.S., 101 S. Ct. 677, 66 L. Ed. 2d 584 (1981)

NATURE OF CASE: Appeal from denial of privilege in tax investigation.

FACT SUMMARY: Upjohn (D) claimed the I.R.S. was not entitled to production of its questionnaires to and interviews of Upjohn (D) employees concerning possibly illegal payments made by Upjohn (D), as they were privileged communications and an attorney's work product.

CONCISE RULE OF LAW: In the case of a corporation claiming the attorney-client privilege, whether the privilege protects any particular communication must be determined on a case by case basis; the "control group" test does not govern.

FACTS: In January 1976, independent accountants discovered that a foreign subsidiary of Upjohn (D) had made payments to or for the benefit of foreign government officials. Upjohn's (D) general counsel conducted an investigation of these "possibly illegal" payments, which included interviews of all foreign general and area managers, and various other Upjohn (D) employees, and questionnaires to the foreign managers. The I.R.S. conducted its own investigation to determine the tax consequences of the payments. It demanded production of all Upjohns's (D) relevant files, including the questionnaires and memoranda of the interviews. Upjohn (D) claimed these were privileged and also protected as the work product of an attorney in anticipation of litigation. Upjohn (D) appealed the enforcement of the summons. The 6th Circuit affirmed to the extent that officers and employees not responsible for directing Upjohn's (D) actions in response to legal advice were not "clients" whose communications could come within the attorney-client privilege. The case was remanded to district court for a determination as to who was not within the "control group." The district court was not to consider the work product doctrine, which the 6th Circuit found inapplicable to administrative summonses. Upjohn (D) appealed.

ISSUE: In the case of a corporation claiming the attorney-client privilege, does the privilege for any communication turn on whether the employee making the communication was responsible for directing the corporations actions?

HOLDING AND DECISION: (J. Rehnquist) No. The "control group" test adopted by the 6th Circuit, which grants the attorney-client privilege to only those communications made by employees responsible for directing the corporations actions in response to legal advice, frustrates the very purpose of the privilege; this is so because it discourages communication of relevant information by employees of the client corporation to attorneys seeking to render their best legal advice to the corporate control group. Further, it invites unpredictability of application, as those whose communications receive the privilege must play a "substantial role" in directing corporate actions in response to the advice. Thus, in the case of a corporation claiming the privilege, the control group test does not govern; whether any particular communication is privileged must be determined on a case by case basis. Here, the communications in question were made by Upjohn (D) employees to its counsel at the direction of its officers, so that they might get advice from the counsel. Thus, these communications, the questionnaires and notes reflecting responses to interviews, are privileged. Regarding the notes which go beyond recording responses to interviews, Federal Rule 26 offers special protection to work product revealing an attorney's mental processess. While a sufficient showing of necessity can overcome protection as to tangible items and documents, a far stronger showing is required as to material revealing a lawyer's mental impressions. Here, the lesser standard was erroneously applied by the district court to the attorney's memoranda of interviews which went beyond the recording of responses. Reversed and remanded.

EDITOR'S ANALYSIS: Before the Upjohn case, the weight of authority favored the control group test. A broader test that some courts employed extended the privilege to embrace any communication by an employee involving his corporate duties and made at the direction of his corporate employer. This latter test was favored by Burger in Upjohn, although the majority declined to formulate a standard. While avoiding some of the problems of the control group test, the broader test seems to unduly extend the shield of privilege.

NOTES:

UNITED STATES v. ARTHUR YOUNG & CO

677 F. 2d 211 (1982)

NATURE OF CASE: Appeal from order enforcing summons to produce files.

FACT SUMMARY: The IRS sought and received an order enforcing a summons directed to Arthur Young & Co. (D) to produce files relating to their client, and Arthur Young (D) appealed.

CONCISE RULE OF LAW: A work product privilege for accountants exists with respect to the tax accrual work prepared by an independent auditor.

FACTS: Arthur Young (D), a major CPA firm, served as an independent auditor for Amerada Hess Corp. In response to publicity about American companies making illegal payments abroad, Amerada engaged both Arthur Young (D) and a law firm to serve as independent investigators into possible wrongdoings by Amerada. Prompted by the inquiry, the IRS (P) instituted a criminal investigation into Amerada's tax returns for the years 1972-74. In connection with the investigation, the IRS (P) issued a summons to Arthur Young (D) for all its files dealing with Amerada and received an order enforcing the summons. Arthur Young (D) appealed, challenging that portion of the order enforcing the summons with respect to Arthur Young's (D) audit work papers and tax accrual work papers.

ISSUE: Does there exist an independent work product privilege for accountants with respect to tax accrual work papers prepared by an independent auditor.

HOLDING AND DECISION: (Feinberg, C. J.) Yes. When a third party to an audit is involved, the IRS may be required to bear an enhanced burden of showing relevance when seeking documents. When the third party is sufficiently involved in the concerns of the party being audited, however, normal standards of relevance apply. The audit work papers could throw light on the correctness of the returns being investigated and were, therefore, relevant. (Affirmed as to that portion of the order enforcing the summons with respect to the audit work papers.) When able to utilize full and frank disclosure of confidential information with respect to a taxpayer's potential tax liability in the preparation of tax accrual work papers, an independent auditor can assist the taxpayer in complying with his obligations under the Federal Securities Laws. Divulgence of this information to the IRS (P) pursuant to an audit investigation could be extemely damaging to the taxpayer's negotiating position. Thus, a conflict could potentially exist between the interest in fully collecting tax revenues, in part effectuated by the broad summons powers granted to the IRS (P), and the interest in maintaining fair and honest securities markets, in large part effectuated by business compliance with the Federal Securities Laws. Creating a work product privilege similar to an attorney work product privilege, safeguarding the independent auditing process, would help insure full compliance with the Federal Securities Laws without unduly hindering the IRS (P) in its efforts to obtain documents. When the IRS (P) can show sufficient need, for example when there are allegations of fraud, the privilege will give way. In this case, since there were no allegations of fraud or other showing of need on the part of the IRS sufficient to override the privilege, that part of the district court's order enforcing the summons with respect to the tax accrual work papers is reversed. Affirmed in part; reversed in part.

EDITOR'S ANALYSIS: It is estimated that approximately one-third of the states now recognize some sort of accountant-client privilege. The privilege recognized in most of these jurisdictions is quite similar to the traditional attorney-client privilege, protecting confidential communications. It is not clear how many jurisdictions recognize an accountant's work product privilege.

NOTES:

TRAMMEL v. UNITED STATES

Sup.Ct. of U.S.,1980. 445 U.S.40, 100 S.Ct.906, 63 L.Ed.2d 186

NATURE OF CASE: Appeal from convictions for conspiracy to import and importing heroin.

FACT SUMMARY: Trammel's (D) wife agreed to testify against her husband in return for lenient treatment for herself, but Trammel (D) argued he had the right to prevent her from testifying against him.

CONCISE RULE OF LAW: A criminal defendant cannot prevent his spouse from voluntarily giving testimony against him because the privilege against adverse spousal testimony belongs to the testifying spouse.

FACTS: In return for lenient treatment for herself, Mrs. Trammel, an unindicted co-conspirator, agreed to testify against her husband at his trial for conspiracy to import and importing heroin. The district court ruled she could testify to any act she observed during the marriage and to any communication made in the presence of a third person but not as to confidential communications between herself and her husband because they fell within the privilege attaching to confidential marital communications. On appeal, Trammel (D) contended that he was entitled to invoke the privilege against adverse spousal testimony so as to exclude the voluntary testimony of his wife. The court of appeals rejected this contention and affirmed the convictions.

ISSUE: Can a criminal defendant invoke the privilege against adverse spousal testimony so as to prevent his spouse from voluntarily offering adverse testimony against him?

HOLDING AND DECISION: No. Inasmuch as the privilege against adverse spousal testimony belongs solely to the testifying spouse, a criminal defendant cannot invoke the privilege to prevent his spouse from offering adverse testimony against him. The Hawkins case left the federal privilege for adverse spousal testimony where it found it at the time, thus continuing a rule which barred the testimony of one spouse against the other unless both consented. However, since that 1958 decision, support for that conception of the privilege has eroded further and the trend in state law is toward divesting the accused of the privilege to bar adverse spousal testimony. The ancient foundations for so sweeping a privilege involved a conception of the wife as her husband's chattel to do with as he wished, and they have long since disappeared. Nor is the desire to protect the marriage a valid justification for affording an accused such a privilege. If his spouse desires to testify against him, simply preventing her from doing so is not likely to save the marriage. Affirmed.

EDITOR'S ANALYSIS: The Model Code of Evidence and the Uniform Rules of Evidence completely abolished the notion of a privilege against adverse spousal testimony and limited themselves to recognizing a privilege covering confidential marital communications. Several state legislatures have followed suit.

NOTES:

COMMONWEALTH v. CAVALIER

Sup. Ct. of Pa., 1925. 284 Pa. 311, 131 A.229

NATURE OF CASE: Appeal from a conviction of first degree murder.

FACT SUMMARY: Cavalier (D) was charged with murder and pleaded insanity as a defense. On appeal, he (D) objected to the trial court's admission of a medical doctor's opinion that he (D) was not insane, and to its exclusion of the testimony of a lay witness who had concluded, from his conduct while incarcerated at the House of Detention, that Cavalier (D) was insane.

CONCISE RULE OF LAW: Whether or not a medical doctor is competent to offer opinion testimony concerning an individual's sanity and whether facts related by a layman form an adequate basis to justify his expression of an opinion on that same subject are both matters which should be left to the discretion of the trial court.

FACTS: Cavalier (D) was tried for first degree murder. His defense was that, at the time of the murder, which occurred when he (D) was only fourteen years of age, he (D) was incompetent and insane. At trial, the Commonwealth (P) was permitted to introduce the opinion testimony of a medical doctor whose training and experience concerning mental illness were only those of the ordinary physician. The doctor concluded that Cavalier (D) had been competent and sane at the time of the murder. The court excluded, however, the testimony of a matron of the Houe of Detention. She testified to the peculiar behavior exhibited by Cavalier (D) during his incarceration at that facility, but the court, rejecting her opinions to his sanity, concluded that the facts which she had related did not constitute an adequate basis for a layman's expression of such an opinion. From these two rulings of the trial court, Cavalier (D) appealed.

ISSUE: May an ordinary physician's opinion concerning an individual's sanity be admitted into evidence, although the opinion of a layman who related detailed facts and observations concerning that individual is excluded?

HOLDING AND DECISION: Yes. A physician engaged in general practice may be competent to testify as an expert concerning the subject of an individual's sanity. Since it is impractical to articulate any one rule which could prescribe the amount and type of experience required of a physician in order to qualify him to evaluate an individual's sanity, the determination of his competency to offer such testimony is best committed to the discretion of the trial court. Similarly, in considering whether the opinion of a lay witness should be admitted for the purpose of showing whether or not a particular individual was sane, the best practice is to defer to the trial judge. It is he who must decide whether the facts related by the witness constitute an adequate basis for admitting his opinion concerning the individual's sanity. In this case, the court did not abuse its discretion either in admitting the opinion testimony of the doctor or in refusing to admit that of the matron of the House of Detention. Therefore, since no error was committed, Cavalier's (D) conviction must be sustained.

EDITOR'S ANALYSIS: In view of the subjectivity necessarily involved in evaluating the sanity of any individual, it is questionable whether any evidence bearing on that issue deserves to be excluded from consideration. There is little consensus among psychiatrists as to what constitutes insanity or its symptoms. In a sense, therefore, no one is truly an expert on the subject. If jurors are required to make a diagnosis which many trained professionals are loathe to undertake, they should at least have the benefit of all available information, including the opinions of experts and laymen alike. Needless to say, once all available evidence has been received, the jurors may accord each item such weight as it merits.

NOTES:

JOHN HANCOCK MUTUAL LIFE INSURANCE CO. v. DUTTON
585 F.2d. 1289 (5th Cir. 1978)

NATURE OF CASE: Appeal from ruling denying judgment n.o.v. and new trial motions in action to recover insurance proceeds.

FACT SUMMARY: During a domestic quarrel, Mr. Sheley was killed, and John Hancock (D) appealed from a subsequent judgment that awarded the beneficiary accidental death proceeds on the grounds that the court improperly received testimony as to the deceased's state of mind.

CONCISE RULE OF LAW: An ordinary person is a competent witness to testify as to another person's state of mind if the opinion is based on personal knowledge and rational perceptions.

FACTS: After returning from an evening out, the Sheleys began quarrelling, and their daughters, including Bell, became involved in the argument. Their relationship had been marked by frequent, violent quarrels. When Mr. Sheley made a threatening remark to one of the daughters, and began unsheathing a shotgun, Mrs. Sheley shot him. Mr. Sheley knew that she had the pistol, but was said to have remarked to a policeman before he died that "I didn't think she'd shoot me." In a subsequent action to collect the insurance proceeds on the life of Mr. Sheley, Bell was allowed to testify that she did not believe that Mr. Sheley thought that Mrs. Sheley would ever shoot him. A jury found John Hancock (D), the insurer, liable for accidental death proceeds. John Hancock (D) filed motions for judgment n.o.v. and for a new trial, which were denied, and then appealed from the denial.

ISSUE: Can an ordinary person testify as to the subjective state of mind of another person if the opinion is based on personal knowledge and rational perception?

HOLDING AND DECISION: (Clark, J.) Yes. (After determining that reasonable men could have found that on the facts of this case that the insured's death was accidental, the court turned to the question of whether the trial court erred in admitting Bell's testimony as to Mr. Sheley's state of mind.) Where, as here, the witness observes first hand the incident in question, his opinion on the feelings of the parties involved, based upon personal knowledge and rational perceptions, are admissible. To hold that testimony of this sort is conjectural would make it impossible for a jury to reach a verdict where an element of the crime is a person's state of mind. Bell witnessed the incident and knew the parties, therefore the trial court did not abuse its discretion in admitting Bell's state of mind testimony. Affirmed.

EDITOR'S ANALYSIS: Such objections to lay opinions are usually based on some supposed difference between facts testified to and opinions testified to. In reality, however, all testimony by way of eyewitness involves inference, and those statements that are sufficiently concrete in their descriptions are found to be accorded fact status, while others less concrete and specific run afoul of the opinion rule.

NOTES:

MARX & CO., INC. v. DINERS CLUB, INC.
550 F.2d 505 (2nd Cir. 1977)

NATURE OF CASE: Appeal from award for plaintiff for breach of contract.

FACT SUMMARY: In an action under the securities laws, the Fugazys (P) alleged that they had been fraudulently induced into selling the assets for their company to Diners Club (D), and Diners Club (D) appealed a jury verdict against them.

CONCISE RULE OF LAW: Testimony by an expert witness consisting of legal opinions as to the meaning of contract terms and the legal significance of various facts is inadmissible.

FACTS: The Fugazys (P) contracted to sell the assets to their company to Diners Club (D) in exchange for unregistered stock. The Fugazys (P) brought suit, alleging that they had been fraudulently induced into selling, alleging specifically that Diners Club (D) had failed to inform the Fugazys (P) of a takeover bid, and that Diners Club (D) had breached its contractual obligation to use its best efforts to register the Fugazys' (P) stock. During the trial, Friedman, an expert witness for the Fugazys (P), was allowed to testify as to his opinions on the parties' legal obligations under the contract and the legal insufficiency of the defenses of Diners Club (D). The jury found against Diners Club (D), and they appealed.

ISSUE: Is testimony by an expert witness consisting of legal opinions as to the meaning of contract terms and the legal significance of various facts admissible?

HOLDING AND DECISION: (Gurfein, J.) No. Testimony by an expert witness consisting of legal opinions as to the meaning of contract terms and the legal significance of various facts is inadmissible. Testimony concerning the practices of lawyers and others engaged in any particular business may be admissible to enable the jury to evaluate the conduct of the parties against the standards of ordinary practice in that particular business. Testimony consisting of legal opinions and legal conclusions intrudes on the province of the judge to instruct the jury on the applicable law, and upon the province of the jury to evaluate the facts in light of the applicable law. The special knowledge of the judge makes this type of testimony unnecessary at best, and at worst could lead to inferences that an expert in any particular area of the law might be more knowledgeable than the trial judge, an impermissible inference in our system of law. In allowing Friedman to testify as to the legal obligations and positions of the parties under contract was highly prejudicial to Diners Club (D), and the trial court erred in admitting the testimony. Reversed.

EDITOR'S ANALYSIS: The exclusion of legal opinion rests on similar grounds to those used to exclude other types of opinion evidence, that the testimony for one reason or another is unnecessary. In the case of most opinion evidence, it is the province of the jury that is intruded on; in the case of the legal opinion testimony, it is the province of the judge that is intruded on. Note that where a judge's particular legal knowledge with respect to an area of law is limited, for example with respect to foreign law, the courts have always allowed legal opinion to help aid in the law's construction or interpretation.

NOTES:

FRYE v. UNITED STATES

293 F. 1013 (D.C. Cir. 1923)

NATURE OF CASE: Appeal from conviction for second degree murder.

FACT SUMMARY: Frye (D) was not allowed to offer expert testimony on the results of a lie detector test administered to him before trial, and when convicted, appealed.

CONCISE RULE OF LAW: In order for scientific proof to be admissible, the scientific principle from which the proof is deduced must be sufficiently established to have gained "general acceptance" in the particular field in which it belongs.

FACTS: Prior to his trial for second degree murder, Frye (D) was subjected to a lie detector test. Frye's (D) counsel offered the scientist who had administered the test to testify as to the results obtained and also offered to have the scientist conduct a test in the presence of the jury. Both offers were denied, Frye (D) was convicted and appealed.

ISSUE: Does the scientific principle from which scientific proof is deduced have to be sufficiently established to have gained general acceptance in the particular field in which it belongs in order for the scientific proof to be admissible in evidence?

HOLDING AND DECISION: (Van Orsdel, J.) Yes. The general rule with respect to the testimony of expert or skilled witnesses is that when the question involved does not lie within the range of common experience and knowledge, the opinions of witnesses skilled in the particular field involved is admissible if helpful to the understanding of the issue. But scientific testimony can only be admitted with respect to well-established scientific principles. Experimental scientific principles not sufficiently established to have gained general acceptance in the scientific community are not sufficiently well-established to give the principle evidentiary force. In this case, the court concluded that the systolic blood pressure deception test (lie detector test) was not yet sufficiently established among psychological and psychiatric authorities to justify admitting expert testimony as to the results of its administration. The trial court did not err in excluding this testimony. Affirmed.

EDITOR'S ANALYSIS: The "general acceptance" test laid down in *Frye* has over the last decade been subject to much critical analysis, limitation, and modification. Some courts have held that this standard applies only to tests for truthfulness, while others have held that the test only goes to the weight rather than the admissibility of the evidence. In some cases, there has been outright rejection of the test (McCormick on Evidence, 3*rd* Ed., pg. 606). It may be of interest to note that the test as administered in the Frye case was later validated; a third person eventually confessed to the murder.

NOTES:

PEOPLE v. KELLY

17 Cal.3d 24, 130 Cal. Rptr. 144, 549 P.2d 1240 (1976)

NATURE OF CASE: **Appeal from conviction for extortion.**

NOTES:

FACT SUMMARY: **Kelly (D) was convicted of extortion after tapes were made of the extorting voice on the victim's telephone and of Kelly's (D) voice, and the tapes were compared by a police expert who identified Kelly's (D) voice by the comparison and who presented the sole evidence that the voiceprint analysis method of comparison was accepted by the scientific community.**

CONCISE RULE OF LAW: **The foundation for admission of results of scientific tests or techniques cannot be sufficiently laid by only the testimony of an expert witness that such tests or techniques are generally accepted by the relevant scientific community absent a showing of academic qualifications enabling him to express such an opinion.**

FACTS: The police taped telephone calls made to one Waskins threatening him. The tapes were compared by a police expert, Nash, to tapes obtained of Kelly's (D) voice over the telephone. Using a method known as voiceprint analysis, Nash gave the opinion that the voice on the extortion tape was Kelly's (D). Nash testified at Kelly's (D) trial and gave the only evidence on the voiceprint analysis method and the results of his test. Though having no formal degree in the field, Nash stated that the method was generally accepted by the scientific community. Kelly (D) appealed his conviction for extortion on the ground that the prosecution had not established the reliability of the voiceprint analysis.

ISSUE: Can the foundation for admission of results of scientific tests or techniques be sufficiently laid by only the testimony of an expert witness that such tests or techniques are generally accepted by the relevant scientific community absent a showing of academic qualifications enabling him to express such an opinion?

HOLDING AND DECISION: (Richardson, J.) No. It is questionable whether a sole witness is ever qualified to testify to the views of an entire scientific community. When, as here, the witness is a leading proponent of such a scientific technique, more caution is appropriate. Furthermore, in this case, Nash was without a formal degree in the area of voiceprint analysis, despite his extensive work and hours of classroom training. Under these circumstances, the prosecution failed to establish the reliability of the test employed. The foundation for admission of results of scientific tests or techniques cannot be sufficiently established by only the testimony of an expert witness that such tests or techniques are generally accepted by the relevant scientific community absent a showing of academic qualifications enabling him to express such an opinion. Reversed.

EDITOR'S ANALYSIS: In modern practice in progressive jurisdictions, no specific training or education is required of an expert in a given field; rather the court may determine from the qualifications alleged whether the witness is an expert in the field. Formal degrees and licenses are particularly relevant of course. Fields that are not technically "scientific" are not excluded, but the foundation for evidence must satisfy the judge that some specialized knowledge is possessed by the expert and that the field can produce reliable results.

UNITED STATES v. WILLIAMS

583 F.2d 1194 (2d Cir. 1978), cert. denied, 439 U.S. 1117 (1979)

NATURE OF CASE: Appeal from conviction under the federal narcotics laws.

FACT SUMMARY: Williams (D) was arrested and convicted under the federal narcotics laws and appealed, challenging the use and admissibility of spectrographic voice indentification evidence.

CONCISE RULE OF LAW: The test for the admissibility of scientific evidence is a balancing test, weighing the probative value, materiality, and reliability of the evidence against the tendency of the evidence to mislead, prejudice, or confuse the jury.

FACTS: Williams (D) was convicted for selling narcotics in violation of federal law. While being investigated, he was observed taking part in a number of drug transactions, and certain phone conversations with respect to proposed sales of narcotics were taped. After his arrest, Williams (D) gave telephone voice exemplars, which were taped. After a pre-trial hearing, voice analysis was ruled admissible and was in fact admitted at the trial. Williams (D) was convicted and appealed.

ISSUE: Is the test for the admissibility of scientific evidence a balancing test, where the probative value, materiality, and reliability of the offered evidence is weighed against the tendency of the evidence to mislead, prejudice, or confuse the jury?

HOLDING AND DECISION: (Markey, C. J.) Yes. The considerations that apply where the question is the admissibility or nonadmissibility of a particular type of scientific evidence are those that are established generally. The court will weigh the probative value, materiality, and reliability of the evidence offered against the tendency of the evidence to mislead, prejudice, or confuse the jury. In the case here, the court found that the evidence of spectrographic voice analysis had clear probative value and was clearly material with respect to the issue of identification. Application of five different indicators of reliability with respect to scientific evidence generally indicated that spectrographic voice analysis had reached a level of reliability sufficient to justify its use in the courtroom. Also, spectrographic voice analysis was not found to be so inherently misleading so as to require its exclusion, since the evidence was easily comprehensible to the juries, the tapes and charts supplied by the analysis were available for jury inspection, and other safeguards common to all types of evidence in general were present. The trial court properly found that virtually all of the safeguards designed to insure reliability and to prevent misleading of the jury were employed and did not err in admitting the evidence. Affirmed.

EDITOR'S ANALYSIS: The theory behind spectral voice analysis, that the relatively stable speech patterns of a person's voice could be used to identify the person, has always been a controversial one. It should not be surprising to the reader that those courts which still employ the Frye standard of general acceptance generally hold that spectrographic voice analysis evidence is inadmissible. Until the validity of spectrographic voice analysis is more firmly established, the courts will be divided on the admissibility issue.

NOTES:

STATE v. AQUILERA

25 Crim. L. Rep. (BNA) 2189, 47 U.S.L.W. 2737, (Dade County Ct., May 7, 1979)

NATURE OF CASE: Consolidated review of traffic violation cases.

FACT SUMMARY: Various defendents brought motions to suppress or exclude the results of radar speed measuring devices in prosecutions of traffic violations, with both sides presenting expert testimony and exhibits on the reliability of the devices.

CONCISE RULE OF LAW: The reliability of radar speed measuring devices as currently used is not sufficiently established to allow the use of their results as evidence in the prosecution of traffic violation cases.

FACTS: Various defendants brought motions to suppress or exclude the results of radar speed measuring devices in prosecutions for traffic violations, with both sides presenting expert testimony and exhibits on the reliability of the devices.

ISSUE: Is the reliability of radar speed measuring devices as currently used sufficiently established to allow the use of their results as evidence in the prosecution of traffic violations?

HOLDING AND DECISION: (Nesbitt, J.) No. Considerable evidence exists pointing to the potential for error inherent in the radar speed measuring devices themselves, in their use, and in the interpretation of their results. The existence of adequately trained officers who recognize these errors is not a sufficient safeguard to establish the reliability of radar speed measuring devices to a degree allowing the use of their results as evidence in a criminal prosecution. Motions to suppress or exclude granted.

EDITOR'S ANALYSIS: The court had no argument with the validity of the underlying scientific principle, the Doppler effect. Since the issue in the instant case concerned the accuracy of the radar units in operation, it is conceivable that courts in other jurisdictions, taking greater stock in the ability of carefully trained operators and on-site testing to minimize or exclude error, will admit this evidence, with questions as to the accuracy of the results going to the weight and not the admissibility of the evidence.

NOTES:

EEN v. CONSOLIDATED FREIGHTWAYS

120 F. Supp. 289 (D.C.N.D. 1954), aff'd, 220 F.2d 82 (8th Cir. 1955)

NATURE OF CASE: Motion for new trial.

FACT SUMMARY: A deputy sheriff was offered as an expert in investigating auto accidents to testify that Een's (P) car had crossed into Consolidated Freightways (D) lane and caused the collision.

CONCISE RULE OF LAW: Before an expert may testify about a conclusion of fact, the subject of the expert's expertise must be a proper subject for opinion testimony.

FACTS: A car driven by Een (P) collided with a truck owned and operated by Consolidated Freightways (D). Holcomb, a deputy sheriff with over 17 years of experience investigating auto accidents, arrived at the scene first and observed the positions of the vehicles before they were moved. Holcomb also visited the site the morning after. Een (P) brought an action for personal injuries against Consolidated Freightways (D). Counsel for Consolidated Freightways (D), over objections by Een's (P) counsel, was allowed to elicit Holcomb's opinion as to where the impact occurred. Consolidated Freightways (D) prevailed, and Een (P) moved for a new trial, claiming the conclusions as to where the impact occurred were an improper subject for opinion testimony.

ISSUE: Must the subject of an expert's area of expertise be a proper subject for opinion testimony before an expert opinion can be given on that subject?

HOLDING AND DECISION: Note stated in the casebook excerpt.

EDITOR'S ANALYSIS: According to Wigmore, in Wigmore on Evidence 6, 1923 at 21, a proper subject area, is one which would appreciably aid the trier of fact in forming a conclusion of fact. If the subject of a question of fact is one generally known or understood, an "expert" would not be able to add to what the trier of fact already knows and would not be able to state a permissible opinion.

NOTES:

UNITED STATES v. FOSHER

590 F.2d 381 (1st Cir. 1979)

NATURE OF CASE: Second appeal from conviction for bank robbery and assault.

FACT SUMMARY: Fosher (D) was convicted of bank robbery and assault almost entirely on the basis of eyewitness testimony.

CONCISE RULE OF LAW: Expert testimony that does not sufficiently aid the trier of fact in the evaluation of the fact in issue or relating to a subject not reliably analyzed by modern science or beyond the ken of the trier of fact can be properly excluded within the discretion of the trial court.

FACTS: Fosher (D) was arrested and convicted of bank robbery and assault. The first conviction was reversed and remanded to the trial court for a new trial, in which the jury was unable to reach a verdict. At the second retrial, Fosher (D) offered to introduce purportedly expert testimony on the unreliability of eyewitness testimony, since the government's (P) case rested almost entirely on the testimony of two eyewitnesses. The trial court declined to admit the testimony, Fosher (D) was convicted, and he appealed.

ISSUE: Can expert testimony that does not sufficiently aid the trier of fact in the evaluation of the fact in issue or relating to a subject not reliably analyzed by modern science or beyond the ken of the trier of fact be properly excluded within the jurisdiction of the court?

HOLDING AND DECISION: (Coffin, C. J.) Yes. The issues of the admissibility and the propriety of receiving expert testimony rests within the sound discretion of the trial court. Evidence not helpful to the trier of fact in the evaluation of facts in issue is of limited relevance. Eyewitness testimony is sufficiently within the evaluative powers of the trier of fact to make expert testimony as to the reliability of eyewitness testimony useless in adding to the common understanding of the issues before the jury. To admit such testimony would be to invade the province of the jury in the evaluation of facts in issue. Here, the trial court found that the proffered testimony would not assist the jury, because it did not sufficiently focus on the issue in question, and that it would not assist the jury in the common sense evaluation of the issues. The court did not err in refusing to admit this testimony. Affirmed.

EDITOR'S ANALYSIS: Even though the studies indicate that there is a substantial error factor with respect to eyewitness identifications, appellate courts, like the one in Fosher, usually refuse to admit expert testimony on the reliability of eyewitness testimony. A more just result may be obtained in borderline cases, where the prosecution's case turns almost entirely on eyewitness testimony, by a determination of the trial court that expert testimony as to the reliability of eyewitness testimony should be admitted.

NOTES:

UNITED STATES v. JOHNSON

575 F.2d 1347 (5th Cir. 1978), cert denied, 440 U.S. 907 (1979)

NATURE OF CASE: Appeal from conviction for conspiracy to import marijuana.

FACT SUMMARY: In Lipper's (D) appeal from a conviction for conspiracy to import marijuana, Lipper (D) challenged the propriety of the trial judge to allow expert testimony as to the source of the marijuana and the qualifications of this particular expert witness.

CONCISE RULE OF LAW: It is not an abuse of trial court discretion to admit expert testimony as to the source of marijuana or to qualify a witness as to the source of marijuana solely on the basis of his extensive experience with the substance.

FACTS: At Lipper's (D) trial for conspiracy to import marijuana, the government (P) was allowed to qualify de Pianelli as an expert witness as to the source of marijuana, and he was then allowed to give his opinion as to the source of the marijuana at issue in this case. de Pianelli's only qualifications as an expert as to the source of marijuana were that he was a frequent user of marijuana, had often dealt in marijuana, and had been asked on many ocassions before to identify the source of marijuana. He had no special training or education to make such identifications. de Pianelli testified that he had tested marijuana from each importation, and verified that the marijuana had come from Columbia. Lipper (D) was convicted and appealed.

ISSUE: Is it an abuse of trial court discretion to qualify a witness as an expert on the source of marijuana solely on the basis of his extensive experience with the drug and to allow expert testimony as to the source of marijuana?

HOLDING AND DECISION: No. The trial judge has broad discretion in the matter of the admission or exclusion of expert testimony; similarly, the trial judge has broad discretion with respect to the qualification of expert witnesses. Only where clearly erroneous will a trial judge's determinations with respect to these matters be reversed. The subject of the inference here, the source of the marijuana, is not likely to be within the knowledge of the average juror, making testimony on the subject relevant and helpful. Since expertise can be obtained through experience as well as training or education, de Pianelli's extensive experience in dealing with marijuana, including identifications of marijuana by source on several occasions, could qualify him as an expert witness as to the source of marijuana. The claim of an ability to identify the source of marijuana is not so inherently implausible as a matter of law to require the exclusion of testimony on the identifications. The trial court did not abuse its discretion in qualifying de Pianelli as an expert, or in permitting him to testify as to his opinion concerning the source of the marijuana in question. Affirmed.

EDITOR'S ANALYSIS: This case demonstrates the wide latitude that the trial judge has in determining who can be an expert witness and on what subjects. For example, carpenters, plumbers, agents, addicts, and a host of other individuals have been found competent to give expert testimony as to a variety of matters within their own particular areas of expertise.

NOTES:

KNIGHT v. OTIS ELEVATOR CO.

596 F.2d 84 (3d Cir. 1979)

NATURE OF CASE: Appeal from directed verdict denying damages for liability.

FACT SUMMARY: Knight (P) was injured when the door of a freight elevator in her employer's workplace closed prematurely and struck her.

CONCISE RULE OF LAW: To qualify as an expert with respect to design defects in the construction and installation of a machine requires only knowledge of the particular part alleged to constitute the design defect, not knowledge of the design and manufacture of the entire machine.

FACTS: Knight (P) was injured when the door to a freight elevator at her employer's place of work closed prematurely and struck her. She brought an action against Otis (D) on grounds of strict liability, breach of warranty and negligence. She offered the expert testimony of Venable on the issue of whether the unguarded elevator control buttons constituted a design defect. Vendable had background in engineering with special reference to machine guarding and had designed guard buttons for other machinery, but lacked expertise with respect to elevators and elevator design. Citing this lack of expertise, the court refused to allow Venable to testify as an expert on whether the unguarded elevator control buttons constituted a design defect. At the close of Knight's (P) case, Otis (D) moved for a directed verdict in their favor, which was granted, and Knight (P) appealed.

ISSUE: Is an expert witness required to have knowledge of the design and manufacture of an entire machine to testify with respect to design defects in the construction and installation of the machine (as opposed to only having knowledge of the particular part alleged to constitute the design defect)?

HOLDING AND DECISION: (Higginbotham, J.) No. To qualify as an expert witness with respect to design effects in the construction and installation of a machine only requires knowledge of the particular part alleged to constitute the design defect. The general rule, that absent an abuse of discretion, an appellate court will not disturb a trial court's decision on an expert's competence to testify, is tempered with the liberal policy of permitting expert testimony that would aid the trier of fact. To require experts such a high standard of particularized, specialized knowledge of any particular industry in order to testify in litigation concerning that industry would place an enormous burden on plaintiff, to whom the services of experts might not be readily available. Venable's background in engineering, machine guarding, and his previous work in machine guarding and guard button design were sufficient to qualify him as an expert on whether the unguarded elevator control buttons constituted a design defect. Lack of expertise in overall elevator design is something that should go to the weight and credibility of the opinion offered, a matter within the exclusive province of the jury. By excluding the expert testimony on this basis, the trial court invaded the exclusive province of the jury and thus erred. Reversed.

EDITOR'S ANALYSIS: It is important to note that even though liberalilty and flexibility in evaluating the expert's qualifications should be the rule, the trial court still maintains such wide discretion in this area. For an interesting contrast, see Perkins v. Volkswagen of America, Inc., 596 F.2d 681, 682 (5th Cir. 1979), where a specialist in mechanical engineering but with no expertise in designing entire automobiles was not allowed to testify as an expert with respect to automotive design.

NOTES:

PEOPLE v. GORSHEN

51 Cal. 2d 716, 336 P.2d 492 (1959)

NATURE OF CASE: Appeal from conviction for second degree murder.

FACT SUMMARY: Gorshen (D), after being sent home from work by O'Leary, returned to work later that evening and killed O'Leary.

CONCISE RULE OF LAW: The admission of uncontradicted psychiatric testimony for the purpose of consideration by the trier of fact on the issue of the presence of a particular mental state is not conclusive on the issue of the presence of the particular mental state.

FACTS: Gorshen (D) had worked approximately half of his shift one particular evening. He had consumed a large amount of alcohol both before and during his dinner break. O'Leary, Gorshen's (D) supervisor, ordered hm to leave work because he was drunk and engaged in a physical altercation with him, leaving Gorshen (D) in need of medical care. On his way back from the hospital, Gorshen (D) expressed his intent to kill O'Leary, and eventually made his way back to his workplace. When O'Leary again appeared, Gorshen (D), in the presence of police officers, shot and killed O'Leary. At the trial it became known that Gorshen (D) had a good reputation, did not usually drink to excess, and had always gotten along with O'Leary. Gorshen's (D) recollections of the evening were hazy: the only thing he remembered after leaving the hospital was that he had to shoot O'Leary. Diamond, a psychiatrist who had examined Gorshen (D), gave uncontradicted testimony that Gorshen (D) suffered from chronic schizophrenic paranoia and stated his opinion that the events of the evening could have been sufficient to develop an obsessive, murderous rage. His opinion was that this rage of Gorshen's (D) eventually led him to kill O'Leary, but that the acts of Gorshen (D) were those of an automaton, lacking any element of intent, deliberation, or premeditation. Gorshen (D) was convicted of second degree murder and appealed.

ISSUE: Is the admission of uncontradicted psychiatric testimony for the consideration by the trier of fact on the issue of the presence of a particular mental state conclusive on the issue of the presence of that particular mental state?

HOLDING AND DECISION: (Schauer, J.) No. The admission of uncontradicted psychiatric testimony for the consideration of the trier of fact on the issue of the presence of a particular mental state is not conclusive on the issue of the presence of that particular mental state. When the specific mental state element of a crime is placed in issue, competent evidence that because of a mental abnormality not amounting to legal insanity an accused did not possess the essential mental state is admissible. Even when insanity is not an issue in the general plea, evidence tending to establish the mental condition of the accused can be properly considered by the trial court to rebut the presence of malice aforethought or itent to kill. Here the trial court properly considered the testimony of Diamond, but the evidence of the objective circumstances surrounding the incident were sufficient to support the finding that Gorshen (D) was guilty of second degree murder. Affirmed.

EDITOR'S ANALYSIS: The use of psychiatric testimony has been greatly expanded beyond its use in presenting clinical diagnoses or evaluations in murder or mental health. Testimony of this type has been admitted on the issues of the accuracy of eyewitness identifications, psychological indicators of deception, truth serums, hypnosis, and profiles of certain types of offenders. (McCormick on Evidence, 3rd.Ed. pg. 622)

NOTES:

UNITED STATES v. STONE

604 F.2d 922 (5th Cir. 1979)

NATURE OF CASE: Appeal from conviction for possession of stolen mail.

FACT SUMMARY: Stone (D) appealed from his conviction for possession of stolen mail on the basis that the government (P) violated the hearsay rule and Stone's (D) right to confrontation.

CONCISE RULE OF LAW: Admission into evidence of extraneous statements on an authentication affidavit constitutes inadmissible hearsay where the affiant is available but does not testify and also violates the defendant's Sixth Amendment right to confrontation.

FACTS: Howard, an employee of the Veteran's Administration and the payee of the stolen check in question, testified that she received her paychecks by mail, that this particular check had never been received, and that the particular check in question was indeed her payroll check. The check had been found in Stone's (D) possession. The government (P) also introduced into evidence a progress sheet with an accompanying affidavit to show that the check had been mailed. Counsel for Stone (D) made objections to extraneous, explanatory statements contained in the affidavit, which were overruled. Stone (D) was convicted and appealed, raising the hearsay and confrontation issues.

ISSUE: Does the admission into evidence of extraneous, explanatory statements on an authenticating affidavit constitute inadmissible hearsay when the affiant is available but does not testify and violate the defendant's Sixth Amendment right to confrontation?

HOLDING AND DECISION: (Thornberry, J.) Yes. When an exparte authenticating affidavit presents evidence beyond the simple authenticating requirements, the extraneous portions constitute inadmissible hearsay. Such an affidavit is not admissible under the public records section when it is solely for the particular litigation where it is offered. Violations of the hearsay rule do not per se establish a denial of the right of confrontation, but where an explanatory affidavit is used as a substitute for live testimony without a showing of unavailability, the right of confrontation is also violated. In this case, there was no showing that the affiant was unavailable, and the trial judge erred in allowing the extraneous statements to be admitted into evidence. Howard's testimony and the language of the progress sheet itself provided such overwhelming proof of mailing, however, that the failure of the trial court to exclude the extraneous statements was harmless error beyond a reasonable doubt, so as not to require reversal. Affirmed.

EDITOR'S ANALYSIS: It is important to note that this procedure of authentication by affidavit does not extend to all public documents under the Federal Rules of Evidence. The certification process provided therein only extends to public records, reports, and recorded documents, all including data complications. (Weinstein's Evidence, Vol. 5, pp. 902-5.)

NOTES:

ZENITH RADIO CORP. v. MATSUSHITA ELECTRIC INDUSTRIAL CO., LTD.

494 F. Supp. 1161 (E.D. Pa. 1980), 505 F. Supp. 1190 (E.D. Pa. 1980), et seq.

NATURE OF CASE: Pre-trial evidentiary opinion ruling on the objections to the admissibility of documents in a massive anti-trust case.

FACT SUMMARY: Consolidated action in which Zenith (P) and NUE (P) alleged that Matsushita (D) and other defendants had conspired to take over the American consumer electronics industry, through the use of techniques and business practices violating the entire range of the anti-trust laws.

CONCISE RULE OF LAW: The notion of authentication is akin to a notion of genuineness, and admissible evidence is required to support a trial court's preliminary determinations on the authenticity of evidence.

FACTS: In 1972, National Union Electric Corp. (P) filed suit against 24 Japanese electronics manufacturers, alleging that they and others had conspired to take over the American consumer electronics products industry. In 1974, Zenith (P) filed a similar action, which was consolidated with NUE's (P) action for pre-trial proceedings. The consolidated action then progressed through discovery under the Manual for Complex Litigation. Essentially, Zenith (P) and NUE (P) alleged that Matsushita (D) and the other defendants had been participants in a conspiracy seeking the destruction of the American domestic consumer electronics products industry in violation of the entire span of anti-trust laws, through illegal price discrimination and the illegal dumping of electronic goods in the United States at less than their fair market value. Matsushita (D) and the other defendants all made motions for summary judgment, some individually, some together, with several dozen motions being filed. In the interest of efficient case management, the court decided to write separately on each discrete legal issue raised. In the considerations of one motion, the court determined that the Sherman Act could be applied against the Japanese defendants (D). The court then considered a host of evidentiary issues in limine in connection with some of the other summary judgment motions, handing down a number of orders dealing with the admissibility of documentary evidence and categorizing the most important documents involved. In a second pre-trial evidentiary opinion in limine, the court ruled on objections to the admissibility of some of these documents based on lack of proof of their authenticity. Among the documents whose admissibility was challenged on authenticity grounds were:

a) The three diaries of Yajinna, an official of the Toshiba (D) Corp.,

b) The diary of Yamada, Department Manager of the Electronic Appliance Department, Consumer Products Division of Hitatchi, Ltd. (D),

c) The diaries of Yamamoto, an employee of Hitatchi, Ltd. (D),

d) The diary of Tokizame, an employee of Matsushita (D),

e) Testimony presented before the Japanese Fair Trade Commission. (JFTC). given in connection with the JFTC investigation in the "Six Company Case," dealing with the business practices of the Japanese firms (D) involved,

f) Minutes of Electronic Industries Association of Japan (EIAJ) Officer's Meeting, and,

g) The EIAJ Statistics Committee 1966 (or the Japan Victor Document), showing that the manufacturers who attended the meeting of the EIAJ Statistics Committee, including defendants (D), agreed to modify their accounting practices to cover up the disparity between home market and export practices. The court then proceeded to resolve the legal evidentary issues raised by the parties, and, after describing the documents involved, applied the legal principles to them to make a determination as to their admissbility.

ISSUE: Is the notion of authentication akin to a motion of genuineness, and is admissible evidence required for the authentication of evidence?

HOLDING AND DECISION: Yes. The notion of authentication is akin to a motion of genuineness, and admissible evidence is required to support a trial court's preliminary determinations as to the admissibility of evidence. A finding of authentication is not similar to a finding of admissibility, the other foundational requirements for admissibility should remain analytically distinct. To require as a standard of authenticity that the proponents must prove that a document is an accurate and reliable account of what the plaintiff wishes to use the document to prove is too high. It subsumes all the issues of many cases under the authenticity issue, and analogy to accepted methods of authentication shows that this is not what was intended under the notion of authentication. Secondly, the requirement of showing authentication falls into the category of conditional relevance. Preliminary questions of conditional relevancy are not determined solely by the judge. For example, it is the jury who will ultimately determine the authenticity of evidence. The court merely determines whether there has been a prima facie showing of authenticity sufficient to admit the evidence. The jury, in determining authenticity, need only show that there is substantial evidence from which they could infer the document's authenticity. As there is no authority anywhere for the motion that the jury could consider inadmissible evidence in this regard, it would be pointless for a judge to rely on inadmissible evidence to fulfill the substantial evidence requirement when the jury cannot consider it. Therefore, the preliminary questions of authenticity should be determined on the basis of whether there is substantial admissible evidence to support a finding that a document is authentic. There are several methods of authentication available, and testimony is not essential for establishing authenticity, and authentication by circumstantial evidence is permissible. Some of the elements which tend to establish authenticity include: (a) the source of a particular document, the method or place of its discovery, and (b) the characteristics of the document itself. (i.e. appearance or contents). Testimony and answers to interrogatories to the extent admissible could be helpful in establishing authenticity, both directly and circumstantially, and a document's similarity to other authenticated as to all of them. The court's reasoning, in part, was that court then reviewed Zenith's (P) foundation and Matsushita's (D) response in light of the applicable legal rules to determine admissibility with respect to each set of documents at issue, ruling as follows on the issue of authenticity:

(Continued on next page)

1) There was sufficient admissible evidence to make a prima facie showing of authenticity with respect to the Yajima diaries, the Yamoda diary, the Yamamota diaries, the JFTC testimony;

2) There was insufficient admissible evidence to make a prima facie showing of authenticity with respect to the minutes of the EIAJ Meeting and the Japan Victor Document; and

3) Except for the testimony in front of the JFTC, all the other evidence had to be excluded since Zenith's (P) showing did not satisfy any of the exceptions under the hearsay rule.)

EDITOR'S ANALYSIS: In a subsequent appeal from the granting of summary judgment in this case, the Circuit Court, in reversing most of the summary judgment granted, held that the trial court had erred in holding that certain documents that were authenticated against some defendant's objections were not authenticated as to all of them. The Court's reasoning, in part, was that once a prima facie case of genuineness is established, the court should regard the documents as sufficiently authenticated against all parties, subject to the right of any party to offer evidence to the ultimate factfinder to the issue of authenticity. See Zenith Radio Corp. v. Matsushita Elec. Indus. Co., 723 F.2d 238 (3rd Cir. 1983)

NOTES:

UNITED STATES v. RATLIFF

623 F.2d 1293 (8th Cir. 1980)

NATURE OF CASE: Appeal from criminal conviction.

FACT SUMMARY: Ratliff (D) was convicted for misrepresenting the value of pre-World War II German bonds used as collateral for a loan because of expert testimony of the real present value of the bonds.

CONCISE RULE OF LAW: An expert does not violate the best evidence rule if the expert does not attempt to prove the content of a writing and if the expert testifies about a document beyond the reach of court processes.

FACTS: Ratcliff (D) exaggerated the present value of pre-W. W. II German corporate bonds which he attempted to use as collateral for a bank loan. Due to the destruction of the German bank during the war, only a portion of the outstanding bonds were redeemable. There was a master list of redeemable bonds in Germany. The government (P) sought to prove the worthlessness of Ratliff's (D) bonds by introducing the testimony of Mintken, a German bond and bank examiner, as to the absence of Ratliff's (D) bonds from the master list. Ratliff (D) challenged the testimony, invoking the best evidence rule, claiming the unavailability of the master list precluded Mintken's testimony. The testimony was admitted, Ratliff (D) was convicted of making false statements to a bank, and he appealed, claiming the court erred, while determining unavailability, in not ruling whether the list was privileged or not.

ISSUE: Is the best evidence rule violated by expert testimony which does not attempt to prove the contents of a writing which is not available through court processes?

HOLDING AND DECISION: (Per Curiam) No. Since Mintken did not try to prove the contents of a writing, which was found to be unavailable, his testimony did not violate the best evidence rule. Mintken's testimony included more than merely observation that Ratcliff's (D) bonds were not on the master list. Rather, he testified as to the bond's status on the list. A ruling on privilege of the list was not necessary as this was only one possible reason for unavailability, and not the one used in this case. Therefore, there was no violation of the best evidence rule. Affirmed.

EDITOR'S ANALYSIS: Testimony that something is not contained in a document is testimony proving the contents of a document and thus is generally inadmissible as hearsay. But the catch-all hearsay exception (described in Federal Rules of Evidence 803(24)) can be used to admit this type of hearsay.

NOTES:

UNITED STATES v. MARCANTONI

590 F.2d 1324 (5th Cir. 1979), cert. denied 441 U.S. 937 (1979)

NATURE OF CASE: Appeal from conviction for armed bank robbery.

FACT SUMMARY: Marcantoni (D) appealed from his conviction for bank robbery on the grounds that evidence relating to serial numbers of the stolen money lacked probative value and violated the best evidence rule.

CONCISE RULE OF LAW: The failure to recover documents in a search pursuant to a search warrant raises a sufficient inference to allow the admission of secondary evidence pertaining to these documents.

FACTS: During a bank robbery, bait money whose serial numbers had been recorded was planted along with the other currency taken. Subsequent investigation by the police led them to the Marcontoni (D) residence. Marcontoni (D) consented to a search of his residence. Detective Brodessor examined currency found at the home and recorded the serial numbers of ten dollar bills. Finding the serial numbers of two of the bills matched the serial numbers of the bait money, Brodessor returned to the residence with a search warrant, but failed to find the bills. At trial, Brodesser testified concerning the two bills he had seen at the Marcontoni (D) residence. The Marcontonis (D) were convicted, and they appealed.

ISSUE: Does the failure to recover documents in a search pursuant to a search warrant raise a sufficient inference of unavailability to allow the admission of secondary evidence pertaining to those documents?

HOLDING AND DECISION: (Tjoflat, J.) The failure to recover documents in a search pursuant to a search warrant raises a sufficient inference of unavailability to allow the admission of secondary evidence pertaining to those documents. In order to satisfy the best evidence rule, it must be found that the documents were lost or had been destroyed, could not be obtained by available judicial procedures, were not closely related to a controlling issue, or that at the time the original was in the possession of the party against whom it was offered, he/she was put on notice that the contents of the document would be a subject of proof at trial, to allow secondary evidence. In this case, the government (P) made no formal attempt to qualify Brodesser's testimony as secondary evidence admissible under the rule, and the trial judge gave no reason for overruling Marcantoni's (D) objections that the testimony was inadmissible. Since it was found on review that the trial judge could have inferred from the fact that the search warrant failed to turn up the two bills, that the documents had been lost or destroyed, the trial court's decision to receive the evidence was correct. Affirmed.

EDITOR'S ANALYSIS: Since the circumstances in each individual case will determine whether loss or destruction will be inferred from one successful search, nearly all jurisdictions give the trial judge a degree of discretion in determining the preliminary question of whether it is feasible to produce the original document. The general standard seems to be whether the search was reasonably thorough and diligent in light of what the particular situation might dictate.

NOTES:

UNITED STATES v. TAYLOR

648 F.2d 565 (9th Cir. 1981)

NATURE OF CASE: Appeal from conviction for wire fraud involving fraudulent loan acquisition.

FACT SUMMARY: Taylor (D) and Wittman (D) induced Continental Bank to make a substantial loan to Wittman's (D) corporation by falsely representing to the bank that Home Federal, Taylor's (D) employer, held a first lien on certain California property.

CONCISE RULE OF LAW: Secondary evidence to prove the contents of a writing is admissible when the original writing cannot be obtained by available judicial procedures.

FACTS: Taylor (D) was indicted for his part in an alleged scheme to fraudulently acquire a substantial loan by making false representations of several material facts. In a letter dated January 16, 1975, Taylor (D) represented that Home Federal held a first lien on certain California real property. The letter was telecopied from San Diego to Wittman (D) in Houston, who photocopied it and sent the photocopy to the bank. On January 24, 1975, Taylor (D) signed a letter of agreement confirming Home Federal's lein, and the loan to Wittman (D) was made. Several months later, Wittman (D) defaulted. At trial, an issue was raised as to one element of the charged offense, interstate communication to execute fraud. It could not be proven conclusively whether Taylor (D) signed the letter in Texas or California. The trial court allowed the government (P) to introduce into evidence Exhibit 24, a photocopy of the letter dated January 16, 1975, on the government's (P) claim that the original had been unsuccessfully supoenaed from the relevant parties. Counsel for Taylor (D) did not object to the original document's unavailability. It was never established that Exhibit 24 was a direct copy of the telecopy, leaving open to question where the letter was acutally signed. Taylor (D) was convicted, with Exhibit 24 proving to be vital, and he appealed.

ISSUE: Can secondary evidence to prove the contents of a writing be admitted when the original cannot be obtained by available judicial procedures?

HOLDING AND DECISION: (Ely, J.) Yes. Secondary evidence to prove the contents of a writing is admissible when the original cannot be obtained by available judicial procedures. The matter is one within the court's discretion. The government (P) in this case had represented to the court that subpoenas to the relevant parties had failed to produce the original letter. Counsel for Taylor (D) did not object to the introduction of the photocopy and had stipulated the unavailability of the original letter. The court acted properly within its discretion in allowing the admission of the photocopy. Affirmed.

EDITOR'S ANALYSIS: The purpose of the best evidence rule is not to obtain the original document at all costs. The rule only requires that the parties come up with best obtainable evidence as to a document's contents. When reasonably diligent efforts have failed in producing the original document, courts will be fairly lax in their admission of secondary evidence to prove the contents of the original document.

NOTES:

AMOCO PRODUCTION CO. v. UNITED STATES
U.S. Ct. of Apls., 10th Cir., 1980, 619 F.2d 1383

NATURE OF CASE: Action to quiet title to mineral rights.

FACT SUMMARY: Amoco (P) and the government (D) disagreed as to whether the Federal Farm Mortgage Corporation had reserved a one-half mineral interest in certain land it had sold, the original deed having been destroyed and the recorded version in Summit County containing no such reservation.

CONCISE RULE OF LAW: If all originals of a writing are lost or destroyed, Federal Rule of Evidence 1004(1) authorizes the admission of other evidence of the contents of the writing.

FACTS: In Amoco's (P) action to quiet title to certain mineral rights, the central question was whether, as the government (D) claimed, the Federal Farm Mortgage Corporation had reserved a one-half mineral interest in a piece of property it had sold in 1942. The government (D) contended that such an interest had been reserved in the 1942 deed conveying the land to the Newtons. However, the original deed and all copies other than the recorded version kept in the Summit County Recorder's Office were no longer in existence, and the recorded version contained no such reservation. After a summary judgment was granted in favor of Amoco (P), the government (D) appealed and cited as error the trial court's exclusion of all the evidence it proffered bearing on the contents of the 1942 deed. Such exclusion was based on the notion that the recorded version of the deed fell within Federal Rule of Evidence 1005, which authorizes the admission of certified copies of public records, and that it precluded admission of any other evidence of the contents of the deed.

ISSUE: Can other evidence of the contents of a writing be admitted if all the orignals are lost or destroyed?

HOLDING AND DECISION: (J. McKay) Yes. If all originals of a writing are lost or destroyed, Federal Rule of Evidence 1004(1) authorizes the admission of other evidence of the contents of the writing. This is the rule that should have been applied by the court below in dealing with the 1942 deed. The rule covering public documents is simply inapplicable. While certified copies of public documents are admissible, this term encompasses only documents "authorized to be recorded or filed and actually recorded or filed." In this case, it would be the actual record maintained by the public office to which the public document rule would apply, not the original deed from which that record is made. Where, as in the case, the original deed is returned to the parties after it is recorded, it is not a public record—and it is the contents of the deed (not the record made from it) that was at issue. Reversed and remanded.

EDITOR'S ANALYSIS: The Federal Rules of Evidence take the position of the American rule, which holds that the next best evidence of a lost paper is a copy thereof and that if such a copy is available then oral evidence as to the contents of the lost paper is inadmissible. A recorded version of a deed, however, is not necessarily a copy.

NOTES:

UNITED STATES v. SCALES

594 F.2d 558 (6th Cir. 1979), cert. denied, 441 U.S. 946 (1979)

NATURE OF CASE: Appeal from conviction for unlawful conversion and conspiracy.

FACT SUMMARY: Scales (D), who was alleged to have embezzled and misapplied the funds of a local chapter of the Laborer's International Union, of which he was the business manager, objected to admission at trial of a summary exhibit of the charges in his indictment.

CONCISE RULE OF LAW: Evidence consisting of a summary of the charges contained in an indictment and some of the objective proof relating to those charges is admissible within the descretion of the trial court.

FACTS: Scales (D) was indicted for conspiracy to embezzle and missapply the funds of the union's local chapter, of which he was business manager. He was also charged with a number of overt acts, including the improper receipt of payments for expenses, the personal use of union funds, and the taking of interest-free loans of union funds for fraudulent purposes. At trial, the government (P) produced 25 witnesses and 161 exhibits, including Exhibit 145, a summary exhibit of the charges in the indictment and part of the government's (P) proof. Agent Tosi, who prepared the exhibit, testified in connection with the exhibit. Scales (D) was convicted of some of the charges and appealed, claiming prejudicial error in the admission of Exhibit 145 and Tosi's testimony.

ISSUE: Is evidence consisting of a summary of charges contained in one indictment and some of the objective proof relating to those charges admissable within the discretion of the trial court?

HOLDING AND DECISION: (Taylor, J.) Yes. A summary exhibit of the charges contained in an indictment and some of the objective proof relating to those charges is admissible within the discretion of the trial court. It is established that the trial judge has the discretion to submit the indictment to the jury in a criminal case, so long as limiting instructions to the jury that the indictment is not evidence of guilt. Summaries of objective proof relating to the charges involved are admissible where the underlying items of proof are voluminous, making in-court examination inconvenient. Summaries of the indictment itself should not be objectionable so long as it is not prejudicially or inflammatorily worded. The summary in question was merely a summary of the indictment and of some of the undisputed objective evidence presented in terms of the relevant counts in the indictment. Absent were any misleading or conclusory references. It was likely to be helpful to the jury and was in no way prejudicial towards Scales (D). The trial judge instructed the jury as to the limited purpose that the summary could serve. The trial court did not err in admitting the summary exhibit. The trial court did err in allowing Tosi to restate portions of the summary exhibit, since the exhibit was self-explanatory, but this was harmless error not requiring reversal. Affirmed.

EDITOR'S ANALYSIS: One should be careful to distinguish between summaries that merely serve to explain matters already presented to the factfinder and summaries which are themselves being offered as evidence. While the former type requires only that the summary aid the factfinder and not be prejudiced to the parties involved, the latter will require a "foundation establishing the admissibility of the underlying data and the accuracy of the summary." (McCormick on Evidence, 3rd Ed. pgs. 708-709.)

NOTES:

TEXAS DEPARTMENT OF COMMUNITY AFFAIRS v. BURDINE

Sup. Ct. of the U.S., 1981
450 U.S. 248, 101 S.Ct. 1089, 67 L.Ed.2d 207

NATURE OF CASE: **Employment discrimination suit.**

FACT SUMMARY: **Once Burdine (P) established a prima facie case of gender based discrimination, the question became the nature of the burden that thereby shifted to her employer, the Department (D).**

CONCISE RULE OF LAW: **Once a prima facie case of employment discrimination has been established, the burden shifts to the employer-defendant to articulate some legitimate, nondiscriminatory reason for the employee's rejection—and that is all that is required at that point.**

FACTS: Burdine (P) brought an employment discrimination suit against the Department (D) under Title VII of the Civil Rights Act, alleging gender based discrimination. The trial court held that none of the decisions made by the Department (D) had been based on gender discrimination. The Court of Appeals reversed the trial court's finding that the Department (D) had rebutted Burdine's (P) prima facie case of gender discrimination. It reiterated its view that the defendant in a Title VII case must rebut a prima facie case of discrimination by proving by a preponderance of the evidence the existence of legitimate nondiscriminatory reasons for the employment action and that those hired or promoted were better qualified than the plaintiff-employee.

ISSUE: Is the only burden an employer must meet to rebut a prima facie case of employment discrimination that of articulating some legitimate, nondiscriminatory reason for its action?

HOLDING AND DECISION: (J. Powell) Yes. When the plaintiff in a Title VII case alleging discriminatory treatment establishes a prima facie case of discrimination by a preponderance of the evidence, this effectively creates a presumption that the employer unlawfully discriminated. The burden then shifts to the employer-defendant to rebut the presumption of discrimination by articulating some legitimate, nondiscriminatory reason for the employment action it took. The employer is not required to assume the greater burden that the Court of Appeals would place on him. Once the employer-defendant articulates a legitimate, nondiscriminatory reason for its action, the plaintiff-employee then has the opportunity to prove by a preponderance of the evidence that the legitimate reasons offered by the employer-defendant were not its true reasons, but were a pretext for discrimination. Since the Court of Appeals erred in its pronouncement of the burden faced by the Department (D), its judgment must be vacated and the case remanded.

EDITOR'S ANALYSIS: The Court's use of the word "presumption" is unique. In cases involving sex or race discrimination claims, the courts usually couch their decisions in terms of shifting "burdens" without employing that term. In fact, none of the statutes that underlie such cases use the term either.

AUTREY v. HARRIS

639 F.2d 1233 (5th Cir. 1981)

NATURE OF CASE: **Appeal from a denial of surviving child insurance benefits.**

FACT SUMMARY: **Autrey (P) appealed from the denial of her application for surviving child insurance benefits under the Social Security Act, in which she relied upon the presumption of death as established by regulation.**

CONCISE RULE OF LAW: **To rebut a presumption of death of a missing person requires a showing that either the missing person is alive or a rational explanation supported by substantial evidence of the person's disappearance in a manner consistent with continued life.**

FACTS: In 1969, Fisher disappeared while piloting an aircraft. Autrey (P) filed an application for surviving child insurance benefits on behalf of their children in 1970, which was denied. She reapplied in 1976, relying on the assumption of death established by regulation. This was also denied. At a subsequent hearing, the administrative law judge relied on evidence that Fisher had failed to file tax returns, a suggestion that he was trying to avoid child support, and random comments by Autrey (P) and her children that there had been family difficulties, to reach a finding that Fisher had disappeared and changed his identity. The administrative law judge denied the application, and subsequent appeals through the district court affirmed that decision. Autrey (P) appealed the district court's ruling.

ISSUE: Does the rebuttal of the presumption of death of a missing person, where it cannot be shown that the person is alive, require a rational explanation supported by substantial evidence of the person's disappearance in a manner consistent with continued life?

HOLDING AND DECISION: (Per Curiam) Yes. The presumption of death attaches once a sufficient showing that the missing person has been absent from his/her residence and unheard of for seven years. Once the presumption is created, the burden shifts to the agency to rebut it. The burden of the agency requires more than mere conjecture as to possible explanations. If it cannot be shown that the missing person is alive, a rational explanation, supported by substantial evidence, of the person's disappearance in a manner consistent with continued life, is required to rebut the presumption. In this case it was perfectly apparent that Autrey (P) had raised the presumption. The evidence of Fisher's legal, financial, and family problems hardly support a purely speculative explanation of his disappearance, and certainly does not meet the agency's burden of bringing forth substantial evidence to explain the disappearance. The district court erred in affirming the agency's denial. Reversed and remanded with instructions.

EDITOR'S ANALYSIS: The substantial proof test as used in Autrey v. Harris does not require that the party with the burden of proof make a sufficient showing of proof that would require a jury to find in it's favor. All that is required is that sufficient evidence be produced upon which a trier of fact could reasonably find in favor of the burdened party.

SHARP v. COOPERS & LYBRENID

649 F.2d 175 (3rd Cir. 1981)

NATURE OF CASE: Class action for damages in securities case.

FACT SUMMARY: Sharp (P) brought a class action suit against Coopers & Lybrenid (D), claiming that investors had been fraudulently influenced in their investment decisions by alleged omissions and misrepresentations contained in a tax opinion letter prepared by Coopers & Lybrenid.

CONCISE RULE OF LAW: In cases involving reliance, the trial court analyzes the plaintiff's allegations in light of the likely proof at trial, to determine the most reasonable placement of the burden of proof.

FACTS: Sharp (P) and others invested in an oil and gas limited partnership. Sharp (P) and the others brought a class action suit against Coopers & Lybrenid (D), alleging that they had relied on a tax letter, prepared by Coopers & Lybrenid (D), which contained omissions and misrepresentations. The trial judge instructed the jury that the investors were entitled to a rebuttable presumption of reliance. After judgment for Sharp (P), Coopers & Lybrenid (D) appealed.

ISSUE: In cases involving reliance, does the trial court analyze the plaintiff's allegations in light of the likely proof at trial, to determine the most reasonable placement of the burden of proof?

HOLDING AND DECISION: Yes. Normally the plaintiff has the burden of proving all of the elements of his/her case. Being an element to a valid claim does not necessarily assign the burdens of going forward and persuasion with respect to that element to the plaintiff. When reliance is an element of the plaintiff's action, it is clear that in some situations a presumption of reliance in favor of the plaintiff is proper. The presumption of reliance should not be made to turn on whether the defendant's conduct can be characterized as an omission or as a misrepresentation. In reliance cases, the shift of burdens is usually justified by the plaintiff's inability to prove that he/she relied on a material omission. The distinction between misrepresentation and omission cases is not entirely clear, since both types of cases involve difficulties in proving a speculative state of facts, the plaintiff's hypothetical behavior. Also, to allow the presumption of reliance to be made on the basis of the omission/misrepresentation distinction would require a dual jury instruction, with all its attendant difficulties, when both omissions and misrepresentations are present. Therefore, the trial court will analyze the plaintiff's allegations in light of the likely proof at trial, to determine the most reasonable placement of the burden of proof of reliance. In this case, both omissions and misrepresentations are present. The purpose of the opinion letter, which failed to disclose certain facts, was to influence investment decisions. Considering the likelihood that investors would rely on the letter, the presumption of reliance was proper, and Coopers & Lybrenid's (D) burden of rebutting the presumption should not be relieved by the additional presence of misrepresentations. Affirmed.

EDITOR'S ANALYSIS: The underlying basis for decisions dealing with the issue of allocation of the burden of proof with respect to why any particular result is reached is not always clear. The decisional basis for these cases generally turns upon the court's particular interpretation of the motions of policy, fairness, and probable ability to produce evidence, when the decision to assign a presumption or allocate a burden of proof is made.

NOTES:

PLOUGH, INC. v.THE MASON AND DIXON LINES

630 F.2d 468 (6th Cir. 1980).

NATURE OF CASE: Appeal from denial of damages for injury to goods transported by carrier.

FACT SUMMARY: Plough (P) sued Mason and Dixon (D) when a shipment of cans transported by Mason and Dixon (D), which had been delivered by Plough (P) in good condition, arrived in a damaged condition.

CONCISE RULE OF LAW: In common-carrier cases involving damage to goods, once the shipper establishes a prima facie case of carrier liability, the burden of proof with respect to negligence and causation issues shifts to the carrier and remains there.

FACTS: Plough (P) delivered two trailer loads of cans in good condition to Mason and Dixon (D) for transportation. When the shipment arrived, the tops of the cans in each trailer load were discolored, and the shipments were rejected. The contamination in one of the trailer loads was attributed to general dust and dirt, since the trailer had a hole and excessive dirt was found in the trailer. The cause of the damage to the second trailer load was disputed. It was conceded by Plough (P) that the plastic tops used on the cans were conductors, attracting dust and other particles from the air, but Plough (P) claimed that they were treated with an anti-static agent. Mason and Dixon (D) claimed that the sole cause of the discoloration was "inherent vice in the caps in that the anti-static agent used in them was ineffective." No hole or excessive dust or dirt was found in the second trailer. The court concluded that Mason and Dixon (D) should prevail on its affirmative defense of inherent vice with respect to the second trailer, and Plough (P) appealed.

ISSUE: In common-carrier cases involving damage to goods, once the shipper establishes a prima facie case of carrier liability, does the burden of proof with respect to negligence and causation issues shift to the carrier and remain there?

HOLDING AND DECISION: (Lively, J.) Yes. In actions to recover from a carrier for damage to a shipment, the shipper establishes a prima facie case of carrier liability when he shows delivery in good condition, arrival in damaged condition, and the amount of damages. Once the prima facie case is established, it creates a presumption of negligence, not an inference. The burden of proof is then upon the carrier to show both that it was free from negligence, and that the damage to the cargo was due to one of the accepted causes relieving the carrier from liability. This burden of proof is both the burden of going forward and the burden of persuasion, and it remains with the carrier. In the present case, the prima facie case was established without any need to find a hole in the trailer or any excessive dirt. The presumption on negligence should have arisen then, and it was error to require Plough (P) to produce additional evidence that Mason-Dixon (D) had negligently transported the goods in a solid or defective trailer. At no point was it found that the "inherent vice" of the caps was the sole cause of the damage. It was error to place the burden on Plough (P) to prove specific acts of negligence on the part of Mason-Dixon (D). Judgment vacated and remanded for further proceedings.

EDITOR'S ANALYSIS: This case seems to be an example of the trend in federal court to give Congressionally created presumptions stronger force than that carried by an ordinary presumption, in that courts will often appear to shift, as in the present case, the burden of persuasion. The California code provides for the shift of the burden of persuasion when the presumption is based upon a public policy, and not when the presumption merely facilitates issues of proof at trial.

NOTES:

SINDELL v. ABBOTT LABORATORIES

26 Cal. 3d 588, 163 Cal. Rptr. 132, 607 P.2d 924 (1980)

NATURE OF CASE: Action for damages for personal injury.

FACT SUMMARY: Sindell (P) appealed when her complaint for damages arising from injuries resulting from prenatal exposure to a chemical manufactured by Abbot Laboratories (D) and others was dismissed upon grant of Abbot's (D) demurrer, because she could not identify the manufacturer whose product caused her harm.

CONCISE RULE OF LAW: Plaintiffs in tort litigation who through no reason of their own cannot identify the particular defendant whose product caused them harm may be able to shift the burden of proof of causation under an extended form of the "alternative liability" theory.

FACTS: Sindell (P) alleged that she was injured as a result of her mother's prenatal use of the drug DES in connection wih the prevention of miscarriage. It is known that DES can cause cancerous and precancerous growths on women exposed to the drug before birth. These growths manifest themselves after a minimum latent period of 10 to 12 years. Sindell (P) sued Abbott (D) and several other manufacturers of DES on behalf of herself and others similarly situated. Abbott (D) and the other manufacturers demurred to the complaint, and the demurrer was sustained without leave to amend on the ground that Sindell (P) stated she did not and could not identify which defendant had manufactured the drug responsible for her injuries. Sindell (P) then appealed.

ISSUE: Are plaintiffs in tort litigation able to shift the burden of proof of causation under an extended form of the "alternative liability" theory, when through no fault of their own they cannot identify the particular defendant whose product caused them harm?

HOLDING AND DECISION: (Mosk, J.) Yes. The general rule with respect to causation is that the imposition of liability depends upon a showing by the plaintiff that his or her injuries were caused by an act of the defendant or by an instrumentality under the defendant's control. There are exceptions to the rule. The alternative liability theory places the burden of proof of causation on tortious defendants in certain situations. Defendants acting in concert to cause injury to a plaintiff is another theory upon which liability can be based. There is also a theory of industry-wide liability which could obviate the necessity of identifying the manufacturer of the injury-causing instrumentalilty. Under the industry-wide theory of liability, where there is evidence that by acting independently, manufacturers had adhered to an industry-wide standard with respect to the safety of the product, if there was industry-wide cooperation, it could be said that all the defendants jointly controlled the risk. The burden of proving causation could be shifted to the defendants if it were shown by a preponderance of the evidence that the product was manufactured by one of the defendants. In a case where there are a large number of manufacturers, as here, courts generally decline to apply the industry-wide theory of liability. Also, allegations that defendants relied on each other's testing and promotion methods do not state a cause of action for concerted conduct to commit a tortious act. Turning to the alternative theory of liability, joint tortfeasors can be held jointly and severally liable for the whole of the damages. The burden of proof of causation is shifted to the negligent tortfeasors when identification is impossible for the plaintiffs. The theory does not require that the defendant be in a better position to identify the manufacturer of the product than the plaintiff is. In the present case, the difficulty or impossibility of identifying the manufacturer of the DES resulted primarily from the passage of time. Sindell (P) claimed that the defendants should be wholly liable under the alternative liability claim cannot stand. The distinction between the present case and prior cases finding liability was that in the prior cases, all of the parties who were our could have been liable had been joined, whereas in the present case, only 11 of the 200 manufacturers were joined in the suit, and only five participated in the appeal. In this context, by numbers alone the odds that one of those five supplied the DES that damaged Sindell (P) are so remote that it would be unfair to make each defendant exonerate itself. Since Sindell (P) is not at fault in producing evidence of causation, and all defendants produced an identical drug, an extension of the alternative liability theory is appropriate. It would be reasonable to measure the likelihood of any defendant supplying the product in question by measuring the percentage which the DES sold by the defendant bears to the entire production of the drug. By joining the manufacturers that produced a substantial share of the DES that injured Sindell (P), the injustice of shifting the burden of proving causation to the defendants is significantly diminished, and each manufacturer's liability for the injury would be approximately equal to the percentage of DES it produced. Reversed.

EDITOR'S ANALYSIS: Both this extension of the alternative liability and the development of the enterprise theory of liability are attempts by the courts to relieve plaintiffs of the burden of proof with respect to causation in fact issues where it would be inequitable to require it of the plaintiff. Although quite similar in nature, the court, in adopting this new form of alternative liability, instead of relying on the enterprise liability theory, also relieves the plaintiff of the burden of proving concerted action, making suit available when Independent actIng defendants are Involved.

NOTES:

MULLANEY v. WILBUR

421 U.S. 684 (1975)

NATURE OF CASE: Appeal in murder case by state.

FACT SUMMARY: The State (P) appealed a decision that its requirement that a defendant prove that he acted in the heat of passion on sudden provocation in order to reduce a homicide to manslaughter violated due process.

CONCISE RULE OF LAW: Due process requires the prosecution in criminal cases to prove beyond a reasonable doubt facts which are essential in the determination of the degree of criminal culpability involved.

FACTS: The State (P) appealed a decision that its requirement that a defendant prove that he acted in the heat of passion on sudden provocation in order to reduce a homicide to manslaughter violated the due process requirement that the prosecution prove beyond a reasonable doubt every fact necessary to constitute the crime charged.

ISSUE: Does due process require the prosecution in criminal cases to prove beyond a reasonable doubt facts which are essential in the determination of the degree of criminal culpability involved?

HOLDING AND DECISION: (Powell, J.) Yes. Due process requires that the prosecution in criminal cases prove beyond a reasonable doubt facts which are essential in the determination of the degree of criminal culpability involved. Criminal law is concerned not only with pure guilt or innocence, but also with the degree of culpability. A determination that one is guilty or innocent does not render due process inoperable, the loss of personal liberty that could hinge on the degree of criminal culpability found is significant. To hold otherwise would allow a state to undermine many of the interests protected by due process, by simply characterizing them as factors that bear solely on the extent of punishment. Affirmed.

EDITOR'S ANALYSIS: A long history in some jurisdictions was overturned by Mullaney v. Wilbur, in that in many states it was accepted procedure to require the defendant to carry the burden of proof in reducing the degree of a homicide. A broad reading of the case would seem to require assigning the prosecution to carry the burden of persuasion with respect to many affirmative defenses in criminal actions, but later decisions of the court have severely restricted the scope of Mullaney

NOTES:

PATTERSON v. NEW YORK

432 U.S. 197 (1977)

NATURE OF CASE: Constitutional challenge to placement of affirmative defense burden on defendant in murder case.

FACT SUMMARY: Patterson (D) challenged the constitutionality under the Fourteenth Amendment's Due Process Clause of burdening the defendant in a murder trial with proving the affirmative defense of extreme emotional disturbance.

CONCISE RULE OF LAW: A state need not disprove beyond a reasonable doubt every fact constituting any and all affirmative defenses related to the culpability of an accused.

FACTS: Patterson (D) challenged the constitutionality under the Fourteenth Amendment's Due Process Clause of burdening the defendant in a murder trial with proving the affirmative defense of extreme emotional disturbance.

ISSUE: Is a state required to disprove beyond a reasonable doubt every fact constituting any and all affirmative defenses related to the culpability of an accused?

HOLDING AND DECISION: (White, J.) No. A state need not disprove beyond a reasonable doubt every fact constituting any and all affirmative defenses related to the culpability of an accused. Due process has traditionally required that only the most basic procedural safeguards be observed, proof of the non-existence of all affirmative defenses has never been constitutionally required. The constitutional limits beyond which a state may not go center around the presumption of elements of a crime. A state may not presume guilt, it must still prove every element of an offense beyond a reasonable doubt. A state may not shift the burden of proof to the defendent by presumming the ingredient exists upon proof of the other elements of the defense. When no presumption is involved, as in the case of affirmative defenses, the placement of the burden of proof is determined by the legislative branch's balancing of society's interests against those of the accused. In this case, nothing was presumed or implied against Patterson (D). Affirmed.

DISSENT: (Powell, J.) To hold that a state can properly place the burden of persuasion on a defendant with respect to a fact that bears criminal culpability simply because no affirmative fact is presumed against a defendant rests on formalistic rather than substantive distinction. The legislature will be able to shift the burden of persuasion with respect to any factor in a criminal case, as long as references to that factor are contained in those sections of the statute that provide for affirmative defenses. The decision severely undermines the protections afforded by due process as determined in previous cases, and it would have been preferable to simply and directly overrule these precedents.

EDITOR'S ANALYSIS: This formalistic approach of the court, allowing the burden of persuasion to be placed on the defendant as to affirmative defenses, has been severely criticized. With respect to the burden to producing evidence, however, it is clear that this burden may be placed on the defendant with respect to the element of a crime as defined. A defendant may be required to introduce some evidence of the element in question for the issue to be considered by the trier of fact.

NOTES:

YEE HEM v. UNITED STATES

268 U.S. 178 (1925)

NATURE OF CASE: **Appeal from conviction for concealing opium after importation.**

FACT SUMMARY: **Yee Hem (P) challenged the statute under which he was convicted for concealing imported opium with knowledge of its importation, as unconstitutional as violative of due process of law and the compulsory self-incrimination clauses of the Fifth Amendment.**

CONCISE RULE OF LAW: **The presumption of innocence may be overcome not only by direct proof, but also by the existence of facts combined with the additional weight of a countervailing legislative presumption.**

FACTS: Yee Hem (P) was found in possession of and concealing a quantity of smoking opium. The statute under which he was prosecuted created statutory presumptions of guilt upon a showing of possession of opium, and as to the source of the opium. These presumptions shift the burden of proof to the defendant to show lawful possession or that the opium was not imported. Yee Hem (P) challenged the constitutionality of the statute, claiming violation of the due process of law and the compulsory self-incrimination clauses of the Fifth Amendment.

ISSUE: Can the presumption of innocence in criminal cases be overcome not only by direct proof, but also by the existence of facts combined with the additional weight of a countervailing legislative presumption?

HOLDING AND DECISION: (Sutherland, J.) Yes. The presumption of innocence in criminal cases may be overcome not only by direct proof, but also by the existence of facts combined with the additional weight of a countervailing legislative presumption. The presumption of innocence is merely a starting point. Where the countervailing legislative presumptions are not arbitrary or unreasonable, the fact that the legislature has given the facts from which the presumption is drawn an enhanced value does not distinguish this situation from what happens in respect to a great variety of presumptions not resting upon statute. Here, the statutory presumptions were not unreasonable or arbitrary. Universal sentiment and settled policy have condemned the non-medicinal use of opium. The use of the countervailing legislative presumption, so long as reasonable and non-arbitrary, does not violate due process or the clause against compulsory self-incrimination. The statute in and of itself compels nothing. The force that one might feel arises from the circumstances of the particular case, not the statute. Affirmed.

EDITOR'S ANALYSIS: The standard arbitrariness or unreasonableness with respect to legislatively-created mandatory presumptions in criminal cases is no longer followed. Such mandatory presumptions will be rigidly scrutinized, and require that "a rational juror could find the presumed fact beyond a reasonable doubt from the basic facts." See McCormick on Evidence, 3rd Ed. pg. 997 (1984).

NOTES:

GRIFFIN v. CALIFORNIA

380 U.S. 609, 85 S.Ct. 1229, 14 L.Ed. 2d 106 (1965)

NATURE OF CASE: Certiorari from a murder conviction.

FACT SUMMARY: Griffin (D), during his trial for first degree murder, did not testify on the issue of his guilt, and both the prosecutor and judge subsequently commented on this failure to the jury, before it convicted him.

CONCISE RULE OF LAW: The Fifth Amendment Self-Incrimination clause implicitly forbids comment by the prosecution on an accused's failure to testify, or instructions by the court that such failure is evidence of guilt.

FACTS: Griffin (D) refused to testify at his trial for first degree murder, invoking the Fifth Amendment privilege against self-incrimination. Before the jury deliberated on the issue of guilt, the prosecutor commented on this failure to testify and suggested that guilt should be inferred therefrom. During instructions to the jury, the court stated that if Griffin (D) failed to explain facts within his knowledge which tended to indicate his guilt, then the jury could take that failure as "tending to indicate the truth of such evidence," but that such failure alone does not by itself "warrant an inference of guilt." Upon conviction, and affirmance of that conviction by the California Supreme Court, Griffin (D) brought a petition for certiorari to this court.

ISSUE: Does comment by a judge or prosecutor on an accused's failure to testify violate his Fifth Amendment privilege against self-incrimination?

HOLDING AND DECISION: Yes. The Fifth Amendment Self-Incrimination clause forbids comment by the prosecution on an accused's failure to testify, or instructions by the court that such failure is evidence of guilt. Such comment by the prosecution or court is a "remnant of the inquisitorial system of criminal justice which the Fifth Amendment protects against." Such comment penalizes the exercise of a constitutional privilege to refrain from self-incrimination and, as such, cannot be allowed. It may be true that there is a natural inference of guilt from a failure to testify as to facts within the knowledge of an accused, but the jury must make this inference on its own without comment from the court. Here, therefore, Griffin's (D) conviction must be reversed.

CONCURRENCE: (Justice Harlan) Although there is no escape from today's decision, since this court has previously held that the Fifth Amendment applies to the States in all its refinements, the decision exemplifies the "creeping paralysis" of the federal system as a result of the "incorporation" doctrine. The States are being stripped of discretion.

EDITOR'S ANALYSIS: This case illustrates the rule applicable to "direct comment" on an accused's failure to "testify." Note, however, that it does not prevent a prosecutor from commenting on an accused's "failure to offer evidence" on critical aspects of the case. It has been held that a court's comment that an accused's "failure to explain" possession of recently stolen property should be considered in determining whether he knew the goods were stolen, does not violate Griffin (Barnes v. U.S.). Of course, what is considered permissible depends upon the wording of the prosecutor's comments. If he emphasizes an accused's failure to present other evidence instead of the fact that he "personally" offered no explanation, there is probably no violation of Griffin. Note further that Griffin does not prevent a prosecutor from commenting to a jury upon an accused's "refusal to submit to reasonable tests or examinations," the results of which would have been admissible on the issue of guilt or innocence. Note, finally, that Griffin does prevent counsel for one of several co-defendants from commenting on the failure of other co-defendants to testify.

NOTES:

UNITED STATES v. DUBE
520 F.2d 250 (1st Cir. 1975)

NATURE OF CASE: Appeal from conviction for bank robbery.

FACT SUMMARY: Dube (D) appealed from a conviction for bank robbery on the basis that the prosecution had failed as a matter of law to sustain its burden of proving his sanity beyond a reasonable doubt.

CONCISE RULE OF LAW: A criminal defendant is presumed sane, but the introduction of evidence of insanity dispels the presumption and subjects the prosecution to the burden of proving sanity beyond a reasonable doubt.

FACTS: Dube (D) was charged with robbery of a federally insured bank. He did not deny the robbery, but introduced the testimony of a psychiatrist and psychologist that he was insane at the time of the robbery. The diagnosis of insanity by these two witnesses were made five months after the robbery, and were based in large part on a narrative history supplied by Dube (D). The prosecution did not introduce expert opinion testimony, but relied on cross examination and the lay testimony of two bank tellers and Dube's accomplice to rebut his case. Dube (D) was convicted, and appealed on the basis that the prosecution had failed as a matter of law to sustain its burden of proving his sanity beyond a reasonable doubt.

ISSUE: Does the introduction of evidence of insanity dispel the presumption of sanity and subject the prosecution to the burden of proving sanity beyond a reasonable doubt?

HOLDING AND DECISION: (McEmtee, J.) Yes. A criminal defendant is presumed sane, but the introduction of evidence of insanity dispels the presumption and subjects the prosecution to the burden of proving sanity beyond a reasonable doubt. Expert testimony is not conclusive even where contradicted, and it may be rebutted in various ways other than the introduction of countervailing expert testimony. Here, even though expert testimony was introduced to show that Dube (D) was insane, the diagnoses were made five months after the robbery and were based in large part on a narrative history supplied by Dube (D). The weight and credibility accorded to this testimony is for the jury to decide. Rebuttal testimony was presented by the prosecution, and it cannot be said that the evidence in this case was such that a reasonable man must have entertained doubts as to Dube's (D) sanity. Perhaps expert testimony that Dube (D) was sane was the better way to rebut the presumption, but it was not necessary. Affirmed.

CONCURRENCE: (Campbell, J.) There is some doubt that the lay testimony and cross-examination was sufficient as a matter of law to rebut the expert testimony. The introduction of evidence of insanity should not dispel the presumptions completely, however. The presumption should still carry some evidentiary weight, and this weight coupled with the rebuttal testimony supports a finding that sanity had been proven beyond a reasonable doubt.

EDITOR'S ANALYSIS: The court seems to follow a sort of "bursting bubble" theory of presumptions, that the presumption only serves to shift the burden of producing evidence, and that once the evidence is produced, the presumption disappears. This appears to give the presumption little effect and to be of little use in criminal cases where elements must be proven beyond a reasonable doubt.

NOTES:

COUNTY CT. OF ULSTER COUNTY v. ALLEN

Sup.Ct. of U.S.,1979. 442 U.S.140, 99 S.Ct.2213, 60 L.Ed.2nd 777

NATURE OF CASE: **Appeal from a grant of a writ of habeas corpus.**

FACT SUMMARY: **Allen (P) claimed that one of the statutory presumptions that played a part in the trial in which he was convicted for weapons possession was unconstitutional.**

CONCISE RULE OF LAW: **A permissive presumption is constitutional if there is a "rational connection" between the proved fact and the ultimate fact presumed, and the latter is more likely than not to flow from the former.**

FACTS: Allen (P) was one of the passengers in a car stopped for speeding. In looking through the window, an officer spotted a handgun protruding from a purse near a female minor in the car. Two more weapons were found during a search. Allen (P) and the others were convicted for felonious possession of the weapons. A New York statute made the presence of a firearm in a car presumptive evidence that it was in the possession of all persons in the car. It was a constitutional challenge to this presumption that convinced the district court to grant Allen's (P) petition for a writ of habeas corpus. The court of appeals affirmed, holding there is no rational basis for the inference that possession of a gun by all occupants in a car is more likely than not to flow from the gun's presence in the vehicle.

ISSUE: Does the constitutionality of a permissive presumption depend on there being a rational connection between the proved fact and the ultimate fact presumed, as well as the latter being more likely than not to flow the former?

HOLDING AND DECISION: Yes. The test of a permissive presumption's constitutionality is whether there is a rational connection between the proved fact and the fact presumed and if the latter is more likely than not to flow from the former. As applied to the facts of this case, the presumption of possession is entirely rational and meets the aforementioned standards of constitutionality. Here, it was highly improbable that the female minor was the sole custodian of the firearms in question. Her purse was open because the guns were too large to fit within it. The guns were in open view and within easy access of the driver and other passengers. Reversed.

DISSENT: (J. Powell) This presumption violates due process because it does not fairly reflect what common sense and experience tell us about passengers in automobiles and the possession of handguns.

EDITOR'S ANALYSIS: A presumption that was the sale and sufficient basis for a finding of guilt would have to satisfy a more stringent test than one upon which the prosecution can rely as one not-necessarily-sufficient part of its proof. Instead of the "rational connection" test, the Constitution would require that the evidence necessary to invoke the inference be sufficient for a rational jury to find the inferred fact beyond a reasonable doubt.

JAVINS v. FIRST NATIONAL REALTY CORP.

428 F.2d 1071 (D.C. Cir.), cert. denied, 400 U.S. 925 (1970)

NATURE OF CASE: **Eviction action for non-payment of rent**

FACT SUMMARY: **First National Bank (P) brought an eviction action against Javins (D) after he defaulted on his rental payment, and Javins (D) asserted a warranty of habitability defense.**

CONCISE RULE OF LAW: **A warranty of habitability is implied by operation of law into leases of urban dwelling units, and breach of this warranty gives rise to the usual remedies for breach of contract.**

FACTS: First National (P) filed an eviction action against Javins (D), alleging that he had defaulted in payment of the rent. Javins (D) admitted he had not paid the rent, but alleged numerous Housing Regulation violations, claiming to establish a course of conduct of violation of those regulations to Javins (D) detriment. This offer of proof reached only those violations that had arisen since the lease had commenced. The trial court rejected the offer of proof and entered judgment for First National (P). This was affirmed on appeal, where the argument was made that First National (P) was under a contractural duty to maintain the rental units in compliance with the Housing Regulations. Javins (D) appealed from this ruling.

ISSUE: Is a warranty of habitability implied by operation of law into leases of urban dwelling units, giving rise to the usual remedies for breach of contract when the warranty is breached?

HOLDING AND DECISION: (Wright, J.) Yes. A warranty of habitability is implied by operation of law into leases of urban dwelling units, and breach of this warranty gives rise to the usual remedies for breach of contract. In traditional analysis, a lease was a conveyance of an interest in land. Rules governing the interpretation and construction of lease obligations have usually remained rooted in old property law. But application of old property law to lease obligations is inappropriate in leases of modern urban dwelling units. The lessee in these transactions seeks more than an interest in the land, he/she seeks a minimum packages of goods and services, which includes proper maintenance. This bare minimum package is often reflected in a city's Housing Regulations. Contract principles established in other areas of the law, such as consumer protection law, provide a rational framework for the apportionment of landlord-tenant responsibilities. Housing Regulations imply a warranty of habitability, measured by the standards they set out, into leases of all housing that they cover. Reversed.

EDITOR'S ANALYSIS: The court in this case seems to be taking judicial notice of legislative facts in order to support the shift to contract principles in governing the construction and interpretation of lease obligations. There is a much less stringent approach to legislative facts judicially noticed than of adjudicative facts. Neither the federal rules nor the California codes provide for the judicial notice of legislative facts, the purpose being that this more lenient standard of judicially noticing legislative facts will continue to be used.

SMITH v. PRO-FOOTBALL INC.

593 F.2d 1173 (D.C. Cir. 1978)

NATURE OF CASE: Private antitrust action challenging the legality of the National Football League's player draft.

FACT SUMMARY: Smith (P) sued Pro-Football (D) and the National Football League (NFL) (D), claiming the NFL (D) player draft was an unreasonable restraint of trade, damaging Smith (P) in that his ability to negotiate a contract for his services was hampered.

CONCISE RULE OF LAW: Trial court factual conclusions should be set aside only if clearly erroneous on the record, and not on the basis of judicially noticed facts appearing for the first time on appeal.

FACTS: Smith (P), a former professional football player, sued Pro-Football (D) and the NFL (D), claiming that the NFL (D) player draft as it existed when he was drafted was an unreasonable restraint of trade, severely limiting Smith (P) in his ability to negotiate a more lucrative contract. The District Court concluded that the draft as it then existed had a severely anti-competitive impact on the market for players' services, and that it went beyond the restraint reasonably necessary to accomplish whatever legitimate business purposes might be asserted for it. Finding that this was an unreasonable restraint of trade, the court found for Smith (P) and awarded him damages consisting of the difference between what he would have received in a free market for player's services, and what he did receive, trebled in accordance with antitrust law. Pro-Football (D) and the NFL (D) appealed.

ISSUE: Should trial court factual conclusions be set aside if not clearly erroneous on the record, on the basis of judicially noticed facts appearing for the first time on appeal?

HOLDING AND DECISION: (Wilkey, J.) No. Trial court factual conclusions should be set aside only if clearly erroneous on the record, and not on the basis of judicially noticed facts. It is not the appellate court's province to disturb the factual findings of the trial court. When the record evidence lends itself to the factual conclusions revealed by the trial court, these conclusions should be accepted. Here, there was no reason to disturb the factual findings of the trial court. The player draft was found to be anticompetitive in both purpose and effect. The fact that it was designed to facilitate competitive balance between teams has no bearing on its anticompetitive nature with respect to the market for player services. Affirmed.

DISSENT: (MacKinnon, J.) There are many significant facts, as contained in the NFL's Official Encyclopedia History of Professional Football concerning the history and purpose behind the draft, and the peculiar nature of the business of professional football, which lead one to conclude that the effect of the draft upon the ability to negotiate a contract was insubstantial, leaving Smith (D) with no cause of action. The validity of the facts upon which this dissent is based is not questioned, and the rules of evidence provide that judicial notice may be taken at any stage of the proceedings. It was therefore not improper to disturb the factual conclusions of the trial judge.

REJOINDER TO DISSENT: The factual bases, and therefore the legal validity of the dissent is flawed by reliance on personal observation and common knowledge in the community. To base a reversal on a factual source that appeared a year after the trial court's decision is improper and a bit unfair.

EDITOR'S ANALYSIS: Reference to ascertainable facts is clearly within the trial judge's power of judicial notice. Reference can be made to any almanac, dictionary, encyclopedia or any other source of reasonably indisputable accuracy. It is interesting to note that although the court attacks the basis of the facts used in the dissent in its rejoinder to the dissent, no challenge was made to the accuracy of the facts used in support of the dissent's position.

NOTES:

STATE v. TAVONE

446 R.2d 741 (R.I. 1982)

NATURE OF CASE: Motion to vacate portion of bail order.

FACT SUMMARY: Tavone (D), released on bail pending appeal of his conviction of showing an obscene movie for commercial gain, sought to nullify that portion of the order preventing him from showing X-rated movies.

CONCISE RULE OF LAW: Portions of a bail order without any rational relation to the assurance of subsequent appearances and submissions to the court's judgment are invalid.

FACTS: Tavone (D) was convicted and sentenced for knowingly showing an obscene movie for commercial gain. He was released on bail pending appeal. The court, concerned with the erosion of public confidence in the court system, included in the bail order a stipulation that Tavone (D) not show any X-rated movies in his theatre. Tavone (D) challenged that portion of the bail order.

ISSUE: Can stipulations not designed to assure subsequent appearance and submission to the court's judgment be validly included in a bail order?

HOLDING AND DECISION: (Kelleher, J.) No. Portions of a bail order without any rational relation to the assurance of subsequent appearances and submission to the court's judgment are invalid. The primary purpose of bail is to assure a defendant's appearance in court. Concern for the image of the judiciary is commendable, but preventing Tavone (D) from showing X-rated movies does nothing to assure his later appearance in court, and is thus an invalid stipulation in a bail order. Motion granted.

EDITOR'S ANALYSIS: Since the court in this case had taken notice of legislative fact, allowing Tavone (D) to continue to show X-rated movies would erode the public confidence, the appeals court could have decided either way. The judicial notice of legislative facts is governed by a much more lenient rule than is the judicial notice of adjudicative facts, allowing the court a large amount of discretion as to what legislative facts will be noticed.

NOTES:

COMMONWEALTH v. JEWETT

17 Mass. App. Ct. 354, 458 N.E.2d. 769, Further Appellate Review Granted, 391 Mass. 1102 (1984)

NATURE OF CASE: Appeal from conviction for rape.

FACT SUMMARY: Jewett (D) appealed from his conviction for rape on the grounds that the court's exclusion of prior misidentification evidence denied him a fair trial.

CONCISE RULE OF LAW: Although within the court's discretion, where the defendant offers evidence of other crimes similar to the crime alleged, which is of a substantial probative value and will not tend to confuse or prejudice, all doubt should be resolved in favor of admissibility.

FACTS: On October 31, 1979, complainant was raped and Jewett (D) was charged with the rape. Extensive and conflicting testimony was received on the complainant's opportunity and ability to identify Jewett (D). The complainant positively identified Jewett (D) at trial. Jewett's (D) defense was mistaken identity, and he presented evidence that he was with friends enroute to meet friends at the time the rape occurred. Jewett (D) also sought to introduce evidence that five days earlier, he had been misidentified by the victim of another rape case, where he showed it was impossible for him to have been the assailant. The judge excluded the evidence, Jewett (D) was convicted, and he appealed.

ISSUE: When the defendant offers evidence of other crimes similar to the crime alleged that is of substantial probative value and will not tend to confuse or prejudice, should the trial court admit the evidence?

HOLDING AND DECISION: (Rose, J.) Yes. Although within the court's discretion, when the defendant offers evidence of other crimes similar to the crime alleged, which is of substantial probative value and will not tend to confuse or prejudice, all doubt should be resolved in favor of admissibility. The evidence should not be too remote in time, have substantial probative value, and should be closely related to the facts of the case against the defendant. Where justice requires, the trial court's decision can be set aside. In this case, sufficient similarity existed between the two rapes, they were both the same in nature, the closeness of time and place of the incidents, and the nature of the identifications made by the victims, to allow a jury to draw an inference that Jewett (D) was the victim of mistaken identity. The case was to close to hold that the exclusion of the prior misidentification evidence was harmless error. Reversed.

EDITOR'S ANALYSIS: Not all state courts embrace such a lenient standard of admissibility; some will require a substantial proof of probability a third person committed the charged offense, not just the raising of an inference that the defendant had not committed the crime. Some states require a direct connection between the third person and the commission of the offense. See Perry v. Watts, 520 F.Supp. 550 (1981).

DOE v. UNITED STATES

666 F.2d 43 (4th Cir. 1981)

NATURE OF CASE: Appeal from pre-trial evidentiary ruling in rape case.

FACT SUMMARY: Appeals were made when the district court's pre-trial evidentiary ruling held that evidence concerning the past sexual behavior and habits of the prosecutrix was admissible in the rape trial of Black (D).

CONCISE RULE OF LAW: In a rape or attempted rape case, reputation or opinion evidence of the past sexual behavior of an alleged victim of such rape or crime is not admissible.

FACTS: At the pre-trial evidentiary hearing in Black's (D) rape trial, the trial court ruled that the following evidence was admissible: (1) evidence of the victim's general reputation where Black (D) resided; (2) evidence of the victim's habit of calling out and speaking to soldiers at the barracks; (3) evidence of the victim's presence around the barracks; (4) the victim's landlord's allegations of promiscuous behavior on the victim's part; (5) evidence of what a social worker had learned about the victim; (6) phone conversations between Black (D) and the victim; and (7) evidence of Black's (D) state of mind as a result of what he knew of her reputation and from what she had said to him. The government (P) challenged the admissibility of the evidence, and Black (D) challeneged the authority of the Court of Appeals to hear the appeal.

ISSUE: In a rape or attempted rape case, is reputation or opinion evidence of the past sexual behavior of the alleged victim of such rape or assault admissible?

HOLDING AND DECISION: (Butzner, C.J.) No. In a rape or attempted rape case, reputation or opinion evidence of the past sexual behavior of the alleged victim of such rape or assault is not admissible. Reputation and opinion concerning a victim's past sexual behavior are not relevant indicators of the likelihood of her consent to a specific act or of her veracity. Defendants are not constitutionally entitled to present irrelevant evidence. Courts of Appeals only have jurisdiction to review final decisions of the district courts, but this requirement of finality is given a practical construction. Balancing the costs and inconvenience of hearing the appeal against the injustice that might result if jurisdiction to hear the appeal is not found leads to the conclusion that the pre-trial evidentiary ruling was final, giving the Court of Appeals jurisdiction to hear the appeal. Although couched in terms of habit, Items 1-5 held by the district court to be admissible are essentially opinion or reputation evidence of the victim's past sexual behavior and are, therefore, inadmissible, and Black's (D) constitutional rights secured by the Due Process Clause and the rights of confrontation and compulsory process are not violated by the exclusion of this evidence. Item 6, however, is not opinion or reputation evidence, and Item 7, while mentioning the victim's reputation, was evidence relevant to the issue of Black's (D) intent. It was not error to find the evidence contained in Items 6 and 7 admissible. Affirmed in part; reversed in part.

EDITOR'S ANALYSIS: Most all jurisdictions have now enacted some form of "rape shield" law to prevent the unbridled use of character and opinion evidence in sexual assault cases. It is clear, however, that the probative insufficiency of such evidence is not the only reason its use is restricted. The public policy in preventing sexual assaults through encouraging victims to come forward and cooperate in the investigation and prosecution of such assaults requires that the victim be protected against unwarranted attack and intrusion on her character or privacy in the name of due process of law.

NOTES:

PEOPLE v. HUGHES

59 N.Y. 2d 523, 453 N.E.2d 484, 466 N.Y.S.2d 255 (1983)

NATURE OF CASE: Appeal in rape case concerning victim's competency to testify after undergoing hypnosis.

FACT SUMMARY: Prosecutor appealed the decision of the intermediate court of appeals to suppress testimony consisting of a victim's posthypnotic recollections in a rape case.

CONCISE RULE OF LAW: The pre-trial use of hypnosis does not necessarily render a witness incompetant to testify to events recalled prior to being hypnotized.

FACTS: The victim was raped on May 19, 1979. Upon being taken to the hospital, she was unable to describe who attacked her or what had happened, but finally in response to her sister's question as to who attacked her, she responded "I saw Kirk" (D). The police had independently determined that Hughes (D) was a suspect, and the victim's husband learned of this. Subsequent questioning revealed more information, but the victim's recollection was still unclear, and she consented to hypnosis in an attempt to identify her attacker. Land, the clinical psychologist who performed the hypnosis, requested that the police not inform him of any details of the investigation. Prior to the first hypnotic session, the victim's husband told her that Hughes (D) was a suspect. She identified Hughes (D) as the attacker and gave an affidavit to the police identifying Hughes (D) as her attacker. Concerned with prehypnotic suggestion, the victim underwent hypnosis with Goldfarb, a psychiatrist, but was unable to recall Hughes (D) as her attacker. She was able to recall that Hughes (D) was her attacker while under the influence of sodium pentothal, a "truth serum." Prior to trial, Hughes (D) moved to suppress the victim's identification. The trial court ruled in a pre-trial hearing that by substantially complying with a series of standards designed to reduce the potential for abuse and suggestibility in hypnotic procedures, that the prosecution had shown by clear and convincing evidence that the hypnotic procedures employed by Land were not impermissibly suggestive under the totality of the circumstances. The trial court noted the need for corroboration to the greatest extent possible. At the trial, the victim testified as to the events, recalled both before and after the hypnosis, and identified Hughes (D) as the attacker. Corroborating evidence was also introduced. Hughes (D) was convicted and appealed. On appeal, the decision was reversed on the basis that hypnotically produced testimony is not generally accepted in the scientific community and should therefore be inadmissible. They noted, however, that the victim would not be precluded from testifying as to facts recalled prior to hypnosis. The State (P) appealed.

ISSUE: Does the pre-trial use of hypnosis necessarily render a witness incompetant to testify to events recalled prior to hypnosis?

HOLDING AND DECISION: (Wachtler, J.) No. The pre-trial use of hypnosis does not necessarily render a witness incompetant to testify to events recalled prior to being hynotized. Hypnosis is recognized as a procedure having a scientific basis capable of producing useful or beneficial results in limited contexts. Attempts are now being made to introduce hypnotically induced statements as evidence in criminal trials. This use is not sanctioned by the scientific community because hypnosis is an inherently suggestive procedure. Where outside verifications of the statements are not available, there is no currently accepted method for scientifically determining the reliability of hypnotically induced recollection. The law is in a state of flux in cases where hypnosis has been used to refresh or restore the memory of a witness which might have been forgotten, overlooked, or occasionally even repressed following a traumatic event. It has been scientifically demonstrated that hypnosis may produce recollections that contain a mixture of accurate recall, fantasy or pure fabrication, in unknown quantities. It is therefore clear that the results are not generally accepted as reliable by the scientific community. Analogizing to cases of suggestive pre-trial identification, it has not been found necessary to preclude a witness from making an in-court identification on the basis of recollections prior to the suggestive procedure, if there is no reliance on the improper identification. A similar procedure with respect to cases involving the pre-trial use of hypnosis would not necessarily require the exclusion of the witness' prehypnotic recollection. The two aspects of the matter that require inquiry and resolution at the pre-trial stage are the extent of the witness' pre-trial recollection, which would establish the boundaries of admissible testimony, and whether the hypnosis procedure was so impermissibly suggestive as to require the exclusion of in-court testimony with respect to such prehypnotic recollection. The prosecution should assume the burden of demonstrating by clear and convincing evidence that the prehypnotic testimony will be reliable, and there is no substantial impairment of the defendant's constitutional right of cross-examination. The trial court erred in concluding that hypnosis was a reliable means of refreshing recollection, and the appellate court was correct in holding that prehypnotic recollection of the victim was not necessarily precluded. Reversed; new trial granted.

EDITOR'S ANALYSIS: Fear of the use of prehypnotic testimony stems from its unreliability. Hypnosis has been shown to be an inherently suggestive procedure capable of producing false results. In addition, hypnosis could also bolster a person's recollection in erroneous recollections, making cross-examination to impeach or to challenge credibility much more difficult.

NOTES:

FLETCHER v. WEIR

455 U.S. 603 (1982).

NATURE OF CASE: Review of writ of habeus corpus in manslaughter case.

FACT SUMMARY: Weir (D) brought a writ of habeus corpus after his conviction for manslaughter was affirmed in the state supreme court, claiming a denial of due process because the prosecutor used his pre-arrest silence for impeachment purposes.

CONCISE RULE OF LAW: In the absence of the sort of affirmative assurances contained in the Miranda warnings, it is not a violation of due process of law for a state to permit cross-examination as to post-arrest silence when a defendant chooses to take the stand.

FACTS: Buchanan was killed in a fight with Weir (D). Weir (D) fled the scene and did not notify the police. When arrested, he remained silent, even though he was not given Miranda warnings. At his trial for murder, Weir (D) took the stand and claimed self-defense, that the killing was accidental. The prosecutor cross-examined Weir (D) as to his post-arrest silence, why Weir (D) had failed to make any exculpatory statements or to disclose the location of the knife he used to stab Buchanan. Weir (D) was convicted of manslaughter, and the conviction was affirmed on appeal to the state supreme court. Weir (D) then brought a writ of habeus corpus to the federal district court, where it was granted. It was subsequently affirmed by the Court of Appeals and brought to the Supreme Court for review.

ISSUE: Absent Miranda warnings, is it a violation of due process of law for a state to permit cross-examination as to post-arrest silence where a defendant chooses to take the stand?

HOLDING AND DECISION: (Per Curiam) No. In the absence of the sort of affirmative aassurances contained in the Miranda warnings, it is not a violation of due process of law for a state to permit cross-examination as to post-arrest silence when a defendant chooses to take the stand. State procedures need not align themselves with federal procedures so long as the state procedure as a whole remains consistent with the due process of law. The assurances contained in the Miranda warnings make silence after the warnings are given so ambiguous that it has little probative value. It would be unfair to use a government-induced silence to be used against him. Absent this inducement, it should be up to the state to resolve the extent to which post-arrest silence may be deemed to impeach a criminal defendant's own testimony. (Motion of respondent for leave to proceed in forma pauperis granted.)

EDITOR'S ANALYSIS: The court seems to have abandoned the idea that in all cases post-arrest silence is too inherently ambiguous to be used as evidence. But even in the absence of Miranda-type assurance, such silence still seems ambiguous. Although knowledge of the law is presumed in many cases, it seems inconsistent to at least allow an inference of knowledge of the law with respect to the right to remain silent when the federal courts have ordered that defendants be told of that right because they would not know it otherwise.

NOTES:

GARNER v. UNITED STATES

439 U.S. 936 (1978).

NATURE OF CASE: Appeal from admission of grand jury testimony of an unavailable witness.

FACT SUMMARY: Garner and others (D), who were convicted of conspiracy and substantive offenses stemming from the alleged importation of heroin, challenged the admissibility of grand jury testimony of an unavailable witness by writ of certiorari.

CONCISE RULE OF LAW: Not stated in casebook excerpt.

FACTS: Garner et al. (D) were convicted of conspiracy and substantive offenses stemming from their alleged importation of heroin. Robinson was allowed to plead guilty to lesser charges in return for testimony against Garner (D). At trial, Robinson refused to testify, and prosecution introduced his grand jury testimony under an exception to the hearsay rule. Robinson then took the stand and denied the grand jury testimony. The Court of Appeals, on appeal, characterized the testimony of Robinson as not giving the impression that the grand jury testimony was false, but that he was afraid to testify against Garner (D). The Court of Appeals affirmed, concluding the admissibility of the grand jury testimony was not barred because it has strong indicators of reliability. They found the grand jury testimony was sufficiently corroborated by other testimony. Garner (D) brought this writ for review.

ISSUE: Not stated in case exerpted.

HOLDING AND DECISION: Certiorari denied.

DISSENT: (Stewart, J.) The state of federal law as to the admissibility of grand jury testimony when the witness is unavailable is unclear. The fact that the testimony was received in grand jury adds little to it's reliability, only the fact that it was given under oath adds credibility. In this case, even that indication of trustworthiness is missing, since he denied the truth of the grand jury testimony at trial. The Circuit Courts are split on the question of whether grand jury testimony when the witness is unavailable is a hearsay exception, and since the evidence could be critical, certiorari should have been granted to resolve the issue.

EDITOR'S ANALYSIS: The unavailability of a declarant is a generally recognized exception, and a refusal to testify is generally sufficient to support a finding of unavailability; the questions will thus inevitably revolve around the trustworthiness and reliability of the grand jury testimony in each particular case. Until guidance is received, the decisions will also be determined by jurisdiction.

NOTES:

UNITED STATES v. ARTHUR YOUNG & CO.

--U.S.--(1984)

NATURE OF CASE: Appeal from judgment refusing to enforce summons to produce files.

FACT SUMMARY: The Court of Appeals refused to enforce an IRS (P) summons to Arthur Young & Co. (D) to produce files related to its client, and the IRS (P) appealed.

CONCISE RULE OF LAW: No work product privilege for accountants exists with respect to tax accrual work papers prepared by an independent auditor.

FACTS: Aruthur Young & Co. (D), a major CPA firm, served as an independent auditor for Amerada Hess Corp. As part of its duties, Arthur Young & Co. (D) prepared tax accrual work papers. The IRS (P), during an audit investigation, issued a summons to Arthur Young & Co. (D) to produce all files relating to Amerada Hess, including the tax accrual work papers, and received a court order enforcing the summons. Arthur Young (D) appealed, and the Court of Appeals affirmed the order in part and reversed in part. While finding the tax accrual work papers relevant, the court balanced the need to secure the integrity of the securities market with the public desire to gain full compliance with the tax regulations and fashioned a work-product immunity doctrine with respect to the tax accrual work papers. Since the IRS (P) had not demonstrated a sufficient showing of need to overcome the immunity and was not seeking to prove fraud on Amerada's part, the Court of Appeals refused to enforce the summons with respect to the tax accrual work papers, and the IRS (P) appealed.

ISSUE: Does there exist a work product privilege for accountants with respect to tax accrual papers prepared by an independent auditor?

HOLDING AND DECISION: (Burger, C. J.) No. No work product privilege for accountants exists with respect to tax accrual work papers prepared by an independent auditor. Since the tax accrual work papers highlight various aspects of a tax return, they are clearly relevant to a legitimate IRS (P) inquiry into those tax returns. The summons power, necessary for the proper and thorough enforcement of the tax laws, should not be overridden, absent express statutory authorization or substantial countervailing policies. Here, substantial countervailing policies were found by the lower court in the form of protecting the integrity of the securities markets. To protect this policy, an accountant's work product privilege similar to an attorney work product privilege was fashioned to prevent disclosure of the tax accrual work papers. But the two situations are not completely analgous, the independent public auditor has a public responsibility in honest reporting that transcends the employment relationship with its client. This public responsibility is sufficient to assure the integrity of the securities markets, without the need for an accountant's work product privilege with respect to tax accrual work papers. Congressional authorization for the privilege does not exist, in fact legislative intent seems to point to the desire to enfore full disclosure in accord with the summon power. Authority seems to indicate that if the summons power is to be curtailed, it is a job for the legislature, and not the court. The Court of Appeals erred in fashioning the accountant work product privilege with respect to tax accrual work papers. Affirmed in part; reversed in part.

EDITOR'S ANALYSIS: Not all states have adopted a privilege for communications to accountants, and the Court of Appeals in the present case created a new form of privilege for accountants in fashioning the work product privilege. Most of the states that have adopted a privilege for accountants have adopted one for the protection of confidential communications, similar to the attorney-client privilege.

NOTES:

THREE JUVENILES v. COMMONWEALTH

390 Mass. 357, 455 N.E.2d 1203 (1983)

NATURE OF CASE: Motion to prevent grand jury testimony of children against their parent.

FACT SUMMARY: Three Juveniles (P) brought this motion to quash subpoenas compelling them to give grand jury testimony pursuant to an investigation into a possible murder committed by the children's (P) father.

CONCISE RULE OF LAW: No parent-child privilege exists to allow a minor child to refuse to testify before a grand jury investigating possible wrongful conduct on the part of the parents.

FACTS: A grand jury began investigating the possible murder of a missing woman by the children's father. The grand jury sought to elicit testimony from the children (P) concerning the incident, and both the children (P) and the parent objected. Subpoenas were issued, and the children (P) moved to quash the subpoena, claiming a family or parent-child privilege not to testify. The motion was denied, and the children (P) filed a petition seeking reversal of the denial of their motion.

ISSUE: Does a parent-child privilege exist that allows a minor child to refuse to give grand jury testimony pursuant to an investigation of possible wrongful conduct on the part of the parents?

HOLDING AND DECISION: (Wilkens, J.) No. No parent-child privilege exists to allow a minor child to refuse to testify before a grand jury investigating the possible wrongful conduct on the part of the parents. Testimonial privileges are exceptions to the general duty of all people to testify. Although some privileges are based on constitutional rights, they need not be and can be fashioned where the important interests promoted by the privilege outweigh the need for probative evidence in the administration of criminal justice. Most terminal privileges concern themselves with confidential communications, only the spousal privilege involves disqualifications from testifying. But the spousal privilege is restricted only to criminal proceedings, showing the reluctance of the legislature to transcend the important interest in requiring all people to testify. A clear majority of the courts that have considered the question have refused to fashion a parent-child privilege. In the present case, the balance of the public's interest in requiring testimony against the interest in preserving the family unit by barring a child from testifying concerning his parents does not compel the adoption of a parent-child privilege. Petition denied.

DISSENT: (O'Connor, J.) The need and desire of society in the preservation of the family unit has already been established by the recognition of the spousal privilege and the fact that the family members are shielded from liability for hiding family members from apprehension. In the only case where a court has recognized its inherent authority to grant testimonial privileges and also attempted to balance the issues presented in the case, the court fashioned a parent-child privilege. Unemancipated minor children, living with their parents, should not be compelled to testify against their parents in a criminal proceeding, and a privilege should be recognized to protect children from being forced to testify.

EDITOR'S ANALYSIS: The privilege in question is usually considered to be for the protection of the child, to prevent the court from compelling him to testify against a parent. This necessarily involves the balancing of competing interests, and judicial deference to legislative guidance and intent is usually a good course to follow. Such deference may be inappropriate where the interests to be protected belong to a group having very little direct impact on the legislative process. Children comprise such a group.

NOTES: